CW00515648

INTERNATI
SOCIALIS

A quarterly journal of socialist theory

Spring 2000
Contents

Editorial

Issue 86 of INTERNATIONAL SOCIALISM, quarterly journal of the Socialist Workers Party (Britain)

Published March 2000
Copyright © International Socialism
Distribution/subscriptions: International Socialism,
PO Box 82, London E3
American distribution: B de Boer, 113 East Center Street, Nutley,
New Jersey 07110
Subscriptions and back copies: PO Box 16085, Chicago
Illinois 60616
Editorial and production: 020 7538 5821
Sales and subscriptions: 020 7531 9810
American sales: 773 665 7337

ISBN 1 898876614

Printed by BPC Wheatons Ltd, Exeter, England
Typeset by East End Offset, London E3
Cover by Sherborne Design Ltd

For details of back copies see the end pages of this book

Subscription rates for one year (four issues) are:

Britain and overseas (surface):	individual	£14 ($30)
	institutional	£25
Air speeded supplement:	North America	£3
	Europe/South America	£3
	elsewhere	£4

Note to contributors

The deadline for articles intended for issue 88 of
International Socialism is 1 May 2000

All contributions should be double spaced with wide margins.
Please submit two copies. If you write your contribution
using a computer, please also supply a disk, together with
details of the computer and program used.

INTERNATIONAL SOCIALISM ★
A quarterly journal of socialist theory

THE EVENTS in Seattle at the end of last year marked a turning point for a generation of activists. The 'Seattle effect' has reverberated across the globe. John Charlton posted a questionnaire on the internet in the weeks following the protests. The responses he received from people who took part in the Battle of Seattle form the basis of an exciting piece that gives us a taste of the enormity of what really happened when 'we' shut down the World Trade Organisation (WTO). Abbie Bakan explores the background of the Seattle protests by looking at the history of the WTO and the prospects for challenging it. An insight into the intellectual basis of the protests is given by Mark O'Brien, as he looks at the life and work of campaigner and economist Susan George.

THE NEW WORLD ORDER behind the WTO has shown its ugly face in Russia's bloody war against Chechnya. Rob Ferguson provides us with a Marxist analysis of the power struggle in the region and the fight against Russian imperialism. Last year's war in the Balkans was the inspiration for the recent Russian onslaught. Lindsey German revisits the region and gives an overview of the history of the Balkan question in a review of Misha Glenny's *The Balkans 1804-1990*.

THE RUSSIAN CIVIL WAR shook the imperialist powers of the time, but the real story of the Bolshevik victory has been shrouded in myth. Megan Trudell vindicates the strategy and tactics of the Bolsheviks and sets her account of the civil war in the context of the ongoing crisis of the world system.

BOOK REVIEWS in this issue include Robin Blackburn, editor of *New Left Review*, on Chris Harman's *A People's History of the World*, Jim Wolfreys on a newly discovered work by Georg Lukács, unearthed from the Communist Party archives in Moscow, and Judy Cox on David Harvey's account of Marxist economics.

Editor: John Rees. Assistant editors: Alex Callinicos, Chris Harman, John Molyneux, Lindsey German, Colin Sparks, Mike Gonzalez, Peter Morgan, Mike Haynes, Judy Cox, Sally Campbell, Megan Trudell, Mark O'Brien, Rob Hoveman and Michael Lavalette.

Talking Seattle

JOHN CHARLTON

Only a couple of months after the event the word 'Seattle' has acquired a new meaning. It is where 'we' kicked the system. The word pops up in India when power and port workers come out on mass strike against privatisation. 'Is it the Seattle effect?' asks a newspaper. The internet is replete with articles analysing its meaning.

I posted a questionnaire on the internet between November 1999 and January 2000. The responses I received, along with personal testimonies and articles, became the basis of this piece.[1]

That a turning point in the struggle against the excesses of world capitalism should take place in Seattle is not without its ironies. Seattle has been lauded as a hub of the burgeoning economies of the Pacific Rim. A boom town of the 20th century's last quarter, 'Seattle' is almost a metaphor for high-tech consumption. It is the home of Boeing, of Microsoft, and those symbols of galloping consumerism, the Starbucks coffee shop empire and Nike, just down the road. A place to live in grace and comfort. All this explains why the Clinton administration wanted to take the World Trade Organisation to Seattle.

Yet there is a downside. In the liberalisation of the global economy US domination may have may have increased, but millions of American workers have been victims of the shrinkage of basic industry, its relocation and the intensification of exploitation in the workplace. For some time the cynical and corrupt leaders of the labour unions have been under pressure from their members to organise a fightback. They chose

Seattle because their public profiles would be enhanced in the glare of the international media circus surrounding the WTO meeting.

There is another twist which should not be lost. The new millennium was being ushered in by the system's leaders and its media on an extravagant tide of hype. Millions of new shopping opportunities were being heralded via the cyber-supermarket. But their party was ruined in the virtual home of e-commerce.

A fightback starting in Seattle has yet another lovely resonance. The city was the location of the only general strike in US history so far. In 1919, in the crisis following the end of the First World War with the US government attempting to smash the Russian Revolution, Seattle workers struck. Jeremy Brecher wrote:

> *Anger, hope and militance grew as in a pressure cooker. Nowhere did this radicalisation go further than in Seattle. The radical IWW and the AFL Metal Trades Council co-operated in sponsoring a Soldiers', Sailors' and Workingmen's Council, taking the soviets of the recent Russian Revolution as their model.*[2]

This forms a nice backcloth to the events of November and December 1999.

'Think the WTO is bad?... Wait till you hear about capitalism!'— placard

Seattle hit the international media on Tuesday 30 November, but events were moving in the previous week. Mitchel C wrote, 'No matter where you turn, rallies, teach-ins and other events are exploding out of the pavement. I went to the International Forum on Globalisation that occurred Friday and Saturday... Tickets were sold by Ticketron. Around 2,500 people participated, the huge auditorium filled to capacity for two days, 9am to 9pm... Sunday, 1,500 people took to the streets in a wonderfully colourful and peaceful (if raucous) procession, hundreds of giant puppets and mass performance theatre against genetic engineering and the WTO, drummers beating on makeshift instruments, an army of genetically engineered corn, another "army of forested trees, fighting against the evil soldiers of the New World Order".'

Damon, Pittsburgh: I got on a Greyhound bus in Pittsburgh at 3am the morning after Thanksgiving and travelled two and a half days to Seattle to join the protests against the World Trade Organisation. I arrived to see tens of thousands of activists from the widest range of causes I've ever seen in one place, united around a common concern—their desire to have a say in the decisions that affect their lives, otherwise known as democracy.

'The senators who ratified the WTO treaty should be tried for treason'—placard

Bill O, Chicago, Illinois: We were up at 5am on Tuesday 30 November. We had a big day planned. There were two main marches, one leaving from downtown and one from Capitol Hill. I was in the Capitol Hill march. We loaded up all the puppets into trucks and sent the larger ones up the road. On our side we had an Earth Mother puppet whose head was eight feet in diameter. Her head and each of her hands were mounted on a wheeled cart, and her fabric body stretched across the street. We also had a ten foot square rolling 'pyramid of corporate power'. I was dressed in my full clown ensemble. I wore signs on my front and back that read, 'WTO—who elected these clowns?' I normally refrain from using 'clown' as a derogatory term, but I felt justified here somehow. I carried my diabolo with me.

Shawna, Jeff and Corey, Victoria, British Columbia: The Progressive Librarians' Guild banner elicited quite a few comments. Most surprise— all positive. We were quite a novelty. People first looked at the banner, then looked again (just to make sure), and looked us up and down as if to assess what librarians look like outside a library. Finally they would look one of us in the eye, smile or pat us on the shoulder. A child asked his mother who we were and she explained, 'These are the people who make sure Harry Potter stays inside the library.' She looked at us, grinned and added, 'Among other activities, I'm sure.'

Bill O: At 7.30am, the march began and turned towards downtown. The rain beat down on us. As we reached key intersections we saw human chains, lockdowns and tripods start to emerge. The police forced us to turn several times. We wound our way about, around toward the Paramount Theatre, which was the location of that morning's WTO opening ceremony. We found a way over the highway and there we were. The front of the Paramount Theatre was walled in with metro buses. Riot police stood on the other side. We had a tripod and a locked down human chain on the other side of the block. There was a bus blaring music down the block. Protesters got up on top of the bus barrier and yelled at the WTO delegates who made their way around the back of the theatre. For a while I thought that the protesters were going to go over the barrier and confront the relatively few police on the other side, but this did not happen. We set about making blockades so the delegates could not get through to attend the meeting.

'Keep the sweatshop in the sauna'—banner

Jake, Seattle: I found a great protester line to help barricade and actually exchanged with WTO delegates from South Africa (Afrikaner bastard), Egypt, Germany and France. Some delegates discussed the issues of child labour, genetically engineered food etc, in sympathy with our causes. Others were belligerent and got a good rash of chanting, blocking and deriding in mass numbers. The arrogance of some of these folks was unbelievable. They were very outnumbered but still tried to push through us. It was very satisfying to say 'no' to their faces, and there was not one damn thing they could do. The shoe was on the other foot. How does that feel? It wasn't bricks that did it. It was massive peaceful protest after laborious turnout work. It was the most unbelievable feeling to rove the canyons of downtown corporate America completely free from state police authority. Tipped dumpsters blocked every intersection. All walks of life cruised the streets going from one line of police standoff to the next. Before the police gassing and macing rush at nightfall we felt completely safe in unity with the mass of humanity. If the bladder was full, pee on a Nordstrom Christmas display window next to a graffiti artist. Probably less human on human violent crime was committed downtown that day than any other day of the year.

David, Berkeley, California: Tens of thousands of union members marched downtown to join the protest. Having shut down all the ports along the Pacific coast from Alaska to San Diego, union members chanted and waved picket signs as their ranks filled the streets as far as the eye could see. Each union's members marched together, each with its own colour jacket or T-shirt, each carrying banners and hundreds of signs printed for the occasion. Many of the morning's young protestors were visibly impressed by the strength of the numbers and organisation. For Annie Decker, 'The power and size of it made me feel joyful. I was proud that we were together, bringing the WTO into the public eye.'

'Capitalism destroys all life'—placard

Bill O: A trickle of delegates was getting through, however, and teams were dispatched to plug the holes. All around the theatre were lines of riot police. At each of these lines protesters made human chains. The police were not going to let us in, but we were not going to let any delegates in either. Some of the delegates who came up on the line I was in were understanding, a few even had conversations with us. Many were very angry and violent, however. One screamed obscenities at us for ten minutes. We would not be provoked.

Ain't no power
Like the power of the people
And the power of the people
Don't stop!
Whose streets? Our streets!
Whose streets? Our streets!—**street chant**

Peter B: The vanguard of the 'big' march arrived downtown about 1.30pm, occupying the whole street. Although it came in fits and starts, it flowed past my vantage point for 50 minutes before I found my Salem friends and joined them. We looped through a number of blocks of downtown, and then began to head out of downtown a block over from where the march came in. To my amazement, we could see a steady stream still coming in! It was 2.45pm. I left the march and stood on the corner to view the rest of the march. By 3pm the march's end had passed the point at which I could see it entering downtown a block up the street. However, it was still another 20 minutes before the end passed my vantage point. This means that the march that often filled the entire street took about an hour and a half to pass one point. Could that be less than 50,000?

Bill O: At this point the police were doing their best to be cordial and communicative. They talked to the spokespeople for the protesters. They tried to keep the tension down. This was good, but it did not last. As the afternoon wore on it became clear that we were winning. Most of the delegates were unable to make it to the opening of the meetings and they were cancelled. The bus barrier around the Paramount Theatre was removed.

'Brush with direct action. Helps to prevent truth decay'—placard

Peter B: I saw signs for at least these unions: steelworkers, electrical workers, teachers, bricklayers, ILWU (longshoremen), painters, Stanford workers, service employees, Teamsters, sheet metal workers, marine engineers, transit workers, boilermakers, plumbers, steamfitters and refrigeration workers, public service workers of Canada, cement masons, pulp, paper and wood workers, nurses, Canadian Airlines workers, and carpenters.

Steve saw 'United Steelworkers from Milwaukee, Wisconsin, Chicago and Gary, United Autoworkers from the Midwest, International Longshore and Warehouse Union from right down the West Coast, Service Employees International Union from all over, Teamsters from all over, International Association of Machinists mainly from the North

West, and many craft unions—carpenters, boilermakers and sheet metal workers, mainly from the North West.'

Doug Henwood: Togetherness was the theme of the labour rally—not only solidarity among workers of the world, but of organised labour with everyone else. There were incredible sights of Teamster president James Hoffa sharing a stage with student anti-sweatshop activists, of Earth Firsters marching with Sierra Clubbers, and a chain of bare-breasted BGH-free Lesbian Avengers weaving through a crowd of machinists.[3]

> *We don't need no corporations*
> *We don't need no thought control*
> *Lock the delegates in the bathroom*
> *WTO has got to go*
> *Hey, coppers! Leave those kids alone!*—**street chant, after Pink Floyd**

Police riot, mass arrests

Steve, Seattle: There were around 1,000 Seattle Police with many coming in from outlying areas—King County Sheriffs and cops from other cities, perhaps as many as another 1,000. There were also 200 National Guards, who were mostly held in reserve. All the cops were in riot gear—padding, shields, with gas masks on or at the ready. The suppression of free speech and assembly was a conscious policy by the city, state and federal government. The pressure was intense from the Secret Service (since Clinton came to town on Wednesday 1 December) and specifically from Secretary of State Madeleine Albright and Attorney General Janet Reno. Reno demanded that the National Guard be called out. Mayor Schell imposed a 'no protest zone' around the convention centre and hotels where the delegates were staying. There was a 7pm to 7am curfew through wider areas of downtown. The 'state of emergency' declared by Mayor Schell was endorsed by the city council with no effective opposition, and even support from the so called 'progressives' on the council. The police chief tried to claim that 'excesses' by the cops were few and understandable considering the strain they were under. In fact, the 'excesses' were the rule. The government decided to clear out the protesters and punish them for their success on 30 November. In doing so tear gas, pepper spray, rubber and wooden bullets, percussion grenades, clubs and arrests were all allowed and encouraged. Six hundred plus were arrested. The police chased protesters into a residential/business neighbourhood a mile out of downtown with no pretext of defending the convention centre area. This was not an 'excess'. It could have been stopped at any time by city officials and wasn't. It was clear policy.

Bill O: The mood was jubilant, but our work was not finished. I hooked back up with the giant puppets. The organisers with radios were sending us to 'trouble spots' where there was tension brewing or small groups in need of support. We brought the puppets to each of the barriers and I entertained the locked down human chains. Our Earth Mother puppet was so large that its very presence changed the energy of every intersection we came to.

'WTO = global injustice!'—placard

Shawna, Jeff and Corey: The 'legal' AFL-CIO march in which we were participating had originally planned to merge with the direct action people on 5th Avenue before turning round and heading back to Seattle centre... However, in a decision that we considered a betrayal of our frontline comrades, the AFL-CIO organisers detoured the march route...a group of marshals stood in front of a street to block our path towards the direct action protesters. We decided to join the direct action group and continued straight through the line of marshals. We found ourselves in a war zone.

Bill O: In the late afternoon we arrived at a major downtown intersection. The human chain there had already been gassed, but they were holding strong. We rolled up with the puppets and it was clear that there was an attack brewing. Behind the protesters was a police line. Behind them were two more lines in formation, gas masks on and ready. Behind them was a line of mounted police. They were in formation as well. It was clear that this mass of protesters was about to be gassed and sprayed. We brought the puppets in close. My companions started the crowd singing:

> *Step by step the longest march, can be won, can be won*
> *Many stones may form an arch, singly none, singly none,*
> *And with union what we will, can be accomplished still*
> *Drops of water turn a mill, singly none, singly none.*

Drummers and a trumpeter played along. I moved up to the police line and started to do my clown routine, making a spectacle out of myself. The human chain, whose faces had been set in grimaces of fear and apprehension, became relaxed and joyful. A carnival atmosphere quickly developed, attracting TV cameras. It was a surreal sight, the joy of the protesters and the grim, Stormtrooper visages of the police, tensing for attack.

'Teamsters and turtles together at last'—placard carried by Teamster

Bill O: As it happened, however, no attack came. The police in the front started to relax their bodies. I heard one laugh at a bit of my slapstick. A whiff of tear gas from another confrontation floated past, making our eyes water. I waved my hand in front of my face. 'Whoa, was that one of you guys?' I asked the cops. Two broke out laughing. Behind the lines the ranking police officers were having a conference. They pointed in our direction and at the cameras. They ordered the horses and the reinforcements to stand down. They were willing to order their men to attack totally peaceful people but the clown and the puppets were too much for them.

By about five o'clock the protests were winding down. Groups were unlocking and dispersing on their own. People were making plans for the next day. It was dark, meetings were over, and we had succeeded. We were moving the puppets around downtown to bring them back for storage for the night. It was in this context that the 'violence' started. Be clear, the only violence that happened up until this point was from the police, directed at peaceful, non-violent protesters engaged in civil disobedience.

Jon: The police backlash that Tuesday and Wednesday night was atrocious. I witnessed it personally in the residential neighbourhood of Capitol Hill. Cops (on encouragement from Clinton's Secret Service as reported in *Seattle Post-Intelligencer*, our own corporate media) aggressively chased and maced and gassed and clubbed and tackled innocent bystanders, as well as protesters, outside of the curfew police state zone. I was gassed but was too quick to be maced or clubbed. A moderate Republican county councilperson, a local CBS reporter, and a young innocent woman bystander were shoved and gassed, clubbed and arrested, and thrown face down on the concrete and her head stepped on while her arms were pulled back, respectively, in this residential neighbourhood. And yet the police could not maintain control.

'Stop exploiting workers'—steelworkers' placard

Damon: Onlookers began yelling, 'Get ready! They're going to do it! Get ready!' I heard the spray and people began screaming in pain. I was just expecting spray, so I was pretty surprised when I felt one of those big clubs land on the top of my head. The guy behind me took most of the force from the blow so I wasn't hurt badly. I covered my head with my arm and covered my eyes with my hand. As the screams continued it became obvious—even though I couldn't see anything from underneath my bandana—that the cops were not only spraying but beating the people as well. A police officer then grabbed my hand, pulled it away from my face and sprayed me in the eyes with a canister of pepper spray.

Dr Richard Andrea, New York City: The police were using percussion grenades. They were shooting tear gas canisters straight at protesters' faces. They were using so called rubber bullets. These are actually hard plastic. Some of the damage I saw: these plastic bullets took off part of one person's jaw, smashed teeth in other people's mouths. I saw police arrest people who had their hands up in the air screaming, 'We are peacefully protesting!'

Kent, Seattle: We were peacefully marching into downtown from the waterfront. The march was led by Bob Hasagawa, president of the 14,000-strong Teamsters Local 174. He attempted to make a speech at the steelworkers' rally—but they cut him off. So he made a speech from a soapbox where he vowed that if anyone was going to be arrested he would be the first (although he wasn't arrested).The march grew to nearly 1,000 people and it felt like we owned the streets of Seattle—that feeling lasted about ten seconds. From out of nowhere, and from two different directions, the cops came in hard with tear gas and percussion grenades. They split the march into several pieces—one group of 300 and another group of 200. Neither group had broken any laws or even entered into the no-protest zone (although we were trying to take it there). Both were pinned downed by the cops and people were arrested. The cops put us on city buses to be processed. After they filled the fourth bus they ran out of room and let them go. It seems that everyone in the city knew who we were. People lined the streets to cheer us as our bus passed.

'Monsanto: don't eat it. Bite back—defeat it!'—placard

Jon, Seattle: In custody most of the people I met had never been arrested before but were no less militant for it. I was stunned by the level of militancy. There was no question in most people's minds that they were fiercely devoted to solidarity, and that they would do whatever it would take to remain in jail till all our demands were met.

The following were fellow-detainees of Kent from Seattle

Teamster organiser: Young guy, early 30s. Progressive wing of the Teamsters and member of Teamsters for a Democratic Union (reform movement in the Teamsters).
Postal worker: early 30s, active when he was in college but had not been active for years. He got fed up with the world and protested against the

WTO. His arrest was an education for him. He now wants to tear the head off the city, state, and country that had him beaten, tear gassed and arrested. He has become more active in his union as a result of being disciplined at work for being jailed.

Graduate student from University of Indiana: late 30s. Studying agricultural engineering. A native of India, he faces possible deportation six months before he earns his PhD.

Sheet metal worker: late 20s. She helped organise an entire workplace into the sheet metal workers' union

Environmental activist: early 20s, from Arcadia, a Californian city (heavily into Green politics). I talked to him a lot. He asked about the history of the Teamsters and where he could find out more about the labour movement. He wants to hold a meeting in Arcadia about the Battle in Seattle.

Direct Action Network leading activist: early 30s. Helped lead the jail solidarity action.

Amanda, student activist: early 20s. Was arrested with me and on my bus. She was active against the US in Kosovo and the bombing of Iraq.

Mike, graduate student from University of Washington: studying genetics. Mid-20s. His first demonstration ever.

Mobilisation and motives

It seems that between 60,000[4] and 80,000 people participated in the events over the five days.[5] This raises two interesting points. Firstly, a total of some 30,000-40,000 people from *one* region is impressive enough, though not unprecedented. From the Seattle region it is remarkable when we realise its geographical location. The urban area is small and distant from other conurbations. By road, Vancouver is two hours to the north. Portland is three hours and the Bay Area 16 hours to the south. Minneapolis is 30 hours to the east. Organisers cannot rely on a vast influx from adjoining urban centres. Only very well prepared and financed contingents, plus highly motivated individuals, could drop in by air. All this makes a national demonstration in Seattle logistically difficult, and its success all the more startling.[6]

It *is* remarkable just how many came from far and wide. On a conservative estimate of numbers 20,000 people travelled a very long way. Over 3,000 came from Canada—the bulk from Vancouver, but there were even busloads from Ontario 2,000 miles away. Probably more than 10,000 travelled up the coast from Oregon and California. One respondent mentions a 'caravan' from California and another from eastern Canada. There were certainly contingents from, at least, Chicago, New York, Boston, Pittsburgh, Milwaukee, Fort Collins and Denver (Colorado), Hartford,

Kent (Ohio), Bloomington, Knoxville (Tennessee), Nevada, Georgia, Louisiana, Arkansas and Iowa. It speaks of considerable organisation, and there is already plenty of evidence of that.

From January 1999 messages were appearing on the internet. Many, like Sam from the Bay Area, first saw it there: 'Six months prior to the WTO meeting I became aware from the internet that a massive protest was in preparation.' The Direct Action Network and the Anarchist Information Service were very active on the internet but also on the ground, informing and co-ordinating and training. Many people say they heard about Seattle in the summer, and from local sources. Geoff said, 'I heard about it from anarchist circles in the Bay Area.' 'I got an anonymous flyer from some anarchists in Olympia, a small city near Washington,' recorded Steven. 'Postering and media reports,' said Chris from Vancouver. Akio reported, 'On the West Coast activist communities had been abreast of the plans for six months prior to the event. It was widely circulated knowledge that big plans were being drafted.' Ann from Victoria, British Columbia, said, 'I first heard about it in May when a Philippines solidarity activist in Victoria went to a preparatory meeting in Seattle.' Tresa, a 30 year old Seattle teacher, said, 'I was in charge of the Religious School... We ended up having some great classes for the 7th, 8th and 9th graders. The 8th grade teacher in particular had been planning a Holocaust lesson and was wondering how to tie it in with Channukah. We talked about the Maccabees, then I got her to the WTO. The students came in early to class and we ate pizza together so we had a good chance to start conversations then. A number of them had been to demos before school.'

In the summer the Ruckus Society and the Rain Forest Action Network sponsored a training camp in northern Washington. According to Z Magazine 150 activists held workshops which 'ranged from urban climbing and banner making to non-violence training and peacekeeping, scouting, technical lockdowns and blockades, media, website design, street theatre, legal tactics, even drumming.' Throughout the autumn, 'warehouses are being scouted as potential squats. Seattle Food Not Bombs is making preparations to feed the troops. A sophisticated media collective has formed to ensure that the good work of protesters is neither ignored nor marginalised. Low power "pirate" radio activists are communications for the masses, and a network of inconspicuous bike messengers will feed information from the streets to the clandestine transmitters'.[7]

Direct action activists brought an enormous amount to the success in Seattle, but the biggest story was the engagement of labour unions after decades of relative passivity and defeat. The leadership of the AFL-CIO was there in force. Against a background of a long term employer offensive and falling revenues the WTO was a great stage to make its presence felt. With a vulnerable Democrat president in a presidential year, pressure on the wannabes, Al Gore and Bill Bradley, would not be out of place. So they brought their mobilising facilities to bear in a fashion not experienced in recent memory. The AFL-CIO website records that 'union activists, many arriving in more than 200 buses hired for the occasion, began gathering at Memorial Stadium two hours before a 10.30am rally. An estimated 30,000 to 50,000 participants overflowed the stadium and spilled into the adjoining park... More than 50 unions, 25 states and 144 countries were [represented] among the activists.' Many respondents to the questionnaire record that union funds were behind the mobilisation of their cohorts.

The success of the operation depended on grassroots rank and file organisation. Ron Judd, executive secretary of the King County Labor Council (Seattle), said, 'We went into churches, community groups, neighbourhood organisations, environmental meetings, schools, high schools, colleges, universities and labour halls, even in people's homes, to talk to them about the WTO and how it affects their lives'.[8] Tina from Chicago said, 'The first I heard was about the labour mobilisation at a labour organisers meeting in April.' Kent from Seattle records, 'In Seattle anti-WTO groups organised at colleges—and most unions had members organising their co-workers around the WTO. People started talking about the WTO nearly a year ago. The sting of NAFTA is still fresh in the minds of many—so the bitterness was already there.' Jeff, an aerospace worker from Wilmington, Massachusetts, went with 15 members of the North Shore Boston Labour Council. His factory is being relocated to Mexico. 'We were pissed. After seven or eight years working on trade issues in our local union it was not hard to sign up 11 people for the trip. Some great trade unionists in the council came along as well. All of us paid our own way and looked to have some fun as well as do some serious protesting,' he said.

When we consider who the activists were, and what took them to Seattle, we uncover an immense variety of background and personal history. Like Annie from Santa Cruz, several talk of 'a radical family background in terms of fighting capitalism and racism through labour movement organising and civil rights, both communist and anarchist'. Several others record radical, socialist or union family histories, whilst others have activist histories themselves. Sam from the Bay Area says he is '70 plus, a Second World War veteran with many years of participation in union and political activities'. Michelle, a socialist from Toronto, is 37. She has been a political and trade union activist for 20 years, 'from protesting against Anita Bryant in the late 1970s to the Gulf War, the national student strike in 1995, the mass strikes in Ontario in 1995-1997, etc'. Kent is a 29 year old socialist metal worker from Seattle, and six years a political and union activist. Annie is a 21 year old student. She has done 'an AFL-CIO internship, civil disobedience for unions, started a student labour club on campus and done police brutality protests'. Bill O is 24. He writes, 'I have been in Art and Revolution for about a year and a half (in Chicago). I am a clown and an actor by trade.' Anon, 47, is an 'unemployed paralegal, left anarchist Jewish atheist'. Tina from Chicago is 46. She writes, '[I have been] an activist for 30 years, women's movement, anti-war, various (non-electoral) political movements, union for 20 years.' Elizabeth, a student in her early 20s, 'helped organise as a national leader in the North American Ad Hoc Student Coalition for Fair Trade'. Akio is a 24 year old college graduate from Eugene who says, 'Seattle was my introduction to the culture of activism.'

Respondents indicated where they believed the pull to Seattle came from. 'Among the rads and youth,' wrote Akio, 'the environment seemed to be the primary concern, followed pretty closely by human rights, especially sweatshop labour... The AFL's constituency was primarily concerned with labour rights and erecting international child labour laws, and also voiced a significant amount of concern for the environment. In my opinion though, more significant than the variety of issues comprising the protest was the general sentiment that democracy is being replaced by corporate oligarchy.' Elizabeth from Vancouver put it down to the 'threat to public services, including education, threat to democracy and the ability of governments to regulate and create standards, protect labour rights, and safety and environmental standards, more pressure to privatise and on the global South to give up completely on labour, health and environmental standards.' Tina saw 'the extraordinary development of the organised labour movement calling for action in the streets on economic and political issues—first time I remember it happening *ever*.' An anonymous man from Vancouver simply wrote, 'I hate capitalism.'

'I want to tear down borders and democratise corporations. Looked like a good place to do it! Many people wanted to save trees. But most of all I think people are just sick as hell of corporate control. Here (in the States) elections are all bought and paid for by corporate money. Corporations are considered people, with freedom of speech, but are never given the death penalty for dumping millions of gallons of oil into the ocean, or for killing Indians at Bhopal, or whatever,' wrote Steven. Tom's view was this: 'I think some people just want to fuck with the power structures because they resent their parents.' Bill O said he was 'interested in fighting the enormous and growing influence of unaccountable transnational corporations and the human rights and environmental havoc that these monsters promulgate. The WTO is one part of a vast complicated system to recolonise the Third World. Almost any issue can be traced back to the systematised power of capital.'

Thinking Seattle

Surely the very first thing to register about the events in Seattle is their anarchic excitement—the sense, in the often almost breathless accounts, of people experiencing a birth of the new. Amber from Denver said, 'I came here to protest the killing of turtles. I'm going home determined to turn the world upside down.' 'Best thing since…wholewheat bread!' says Tina. For Dean, 'It changed the world and the movement.' Jon says, 'I am still trying to understand it all. I am proud to have been there and feel like we accomplished far more than we could have predicted.' 'I think it made me believe we can actually change things,' writes Albert. And Steve just writes, 'Yeh! Fuck shit up!' 'When can we have another one?' asks Michelle. A locked-out Kaiser aluminium worker said, 'A year ago I thought a redwood deck was the most beautiful thing in the world. Now I understand the importance of sustainability. I guess I'm an environmentalist now'.[9]

From the union bureaucrats paraphrasing Marx to the Lesbian Avenger proclaiming, 'My nipples stand in solidarity with the steelworkers and Teamsters and all the labouring people,' there is a sense of possibility of moving into a new politics with agendas not yet written.

Many demonstrations would throw up an activist profile similar to Seattle in its variety, especially among its organisers and certainly round the environmental issues which have characterised much radical action in the recent past. Yet the best lieutenants cannot build a mass demonstration by themselves. There must be an 'army' ready to respond. That there was speaks of an enormous depth of feeling—a raised consciousness across a significant swathe of society. There have been numerous courageous actions by environmental activists, and a rising level of interest in the issues they constantly raise. A whole generation of high school and college students have been touched, so to speak, by dolphins, giant redwoods, the rain forests, the greenhouse effect and urban pollution. And there are no face masks strong enough to block the stench of corruption at the top.

For workers across the Western world the past quarter of a century has been an experience of retreat and retrenchment, faced with declining wages, rising prices and severe discipline in the workplace. Joe B from Portland expresses it well: 'You go out to work—if you're lucky. Some trumped up bastard tells you the time of day. Your wages go up—but not at the rate of cabbages at WalMart. Then the plant shuts down.' It is this cry that is being heard more and more, but it is still largely hesitant—if angry. The mobilisation for Seattle is the great example, so far, of a shift from awareness and attitude to action.

In one important respect this movement's composition is different from the movement of the 1960s when, by and large, the working class and its labour unions were not involved. In Seattle it is quite clear that the largest contingents were from that constituency. By the end of the event sections of it were in a close and apparently harmonious relationship with the 'natural' constituency of demonstrators: students, environmentalists of several stripes, 1968 veterans and their children.

Much of the media evinced surprise, as if a sort of Berlin Wall existed between the constituencies. This ignores important changes which have taken place over the last 30 years. The working class has not disappeared; its composition has altered. There are new occupations, and old ones have changed. The skilled have been deskilled and whole areas of formerly 'middle class' labour have been subordinated to 'factory-style' routine, discipline and insecurity. At the same time the expansion of education has tipped masses of college graduates, often overqualified, into such jobs. The steadily falling vote in US presidential elections has been one register of the growth of an enormous chunk of the population with a rightly cynical attitude to the official political process. This does not make them conscious revolutionaries overnight. Nevertheless, there are fresh tensions and anxieties to add to permanent ones. Seattle is an example of a popular upsurge, a reaction to such tensions. They are quite thrilling in their capacity to break moulds.

Most people, from all campaigns and groups, went to Seattle with only the vague goal of demonstrating effectively against the disparate excesses of the WTO. The scale of the mobilisation surprised many of them. The crude violence of the law and order machine shocked everyone. Enormous warmth was expressed for the birth of new alliances. Ideas were in the crucible. Labour bureaucrats arriving with a nationalist-protectionist agenda felt the pressure from their audience to mute such positions in favour of an internationalist stance. Jeff, the aerospace worker from Massachusetts, wrote, 'There could be no mistake that this was not a Pat Buchanan crew. This makes building alliances easier, both within the US and across the borders. We've come a long way from thinking that the answer is just to "Buy American".'

David, from Berkeley, California has the last word:

Those who marched or stood or sat in the streets of Seattle this week made history, and they knew it. And like the great marches against the Vietnam War,

*or the first sit-ins in the South in the late 1950s, it was not always easy to see
just what history was being made, especially for those closest to the events of
the time. Tear gas, rubber bullets and police sweeps, the object of incessant
media coverage, are the outward signs of impending change—that the
guardians of the social order have grown afraid. And there's always a little
history in that. But perhaps the greatest impact of Seattle will be on the
people who were there. Just as anti-war demonstrations and civil rights sit-
ins of decades ago were focal points from which people fanned out across the
country, spreading the gospel of their movement, Seattle is also a beginning
of something greater yet to come. What will the people who filled its downtown streets take with them back into this city's rainy neighbourhoods, or to
similar communities in towns and cities across the country?*

Notes

1   I have to thank Albert, Dean, Geoff, Jon, Kent, Steve, Jake and Tresa from Seattle;
    Akio and Steve from Eugene; Ann, Chris and Elizabeth from Vancouver, British
    Columbia; Corey, Shelley, Shawna, and Jeff from Victoria, British Columbia;
    Michelle from Toronto; Bill O and Tina from Chicago; Peter from Kent; Mitchel
    from Brooklyn; Damon from Pittsburgh; Jeff from Massachusetts; Tom, Sam,
    Mark and David from the Bay Area; plus three anonymous respondents. Helpful
    suggestions were made by Abbie Bakan, Colin Barker, Mick Charlton, Nick
    Howard, Steve Leigh, Michelle Robidoux and Sabby Sagall.
2   J Brecher, *Strike!* (San Francisco, 1972), p104.
3   D Henwood, *Left Business Observer* (http://www.panix.com/~dhenwood/
    lbo_about.html), 30 November 1999.
4   No respondent estimated under 40,000. The highest suggestion was over 100,000.
    The best guess is somewhere in the 60,000-80,000 region.
5   Estimates of where people came from varied wildly from 15 percent to 80 percent
    from the Seattle locality, but the majority suggest 50 percent to 70 percent local,
    so we could settle for around 60 percent, or 40,000 people.
6   A WTO conference might easily have been scheduled for, say, Washington DC.
    Given that city's relationship to contingent conurbations down the East Coast we
    might now have been reviewing and assessing a demonstration of upwards of a
    million. The level of local participation at Seattle is therefore very remarkable and
    must surely reflect a new engagement.
7   D Moynihan, *Z Magazine*, December 1999.
8   Report by K Murphy and N Cleeland, *Los Angles Times*, 4 December 1999.
9   D Henwood, op cit.

After Seattle: the politics of the World Trade Organisation

ABBIE BAKAN

Introduction: the Battle of Seattle

History was made the week beginning 27 November 1999. During that week, in the US city of Seattle, Washington, an international meeting of the most powerful corporate interests in the world was to set the stage for the unbridled reign of profit into the new millennium. Canada's senior ranking federal Liberal Party cabinet minister, Pierre Pettigrew, was one of many dignitaries who found their plans suddenly changed. He had been looking forward to the fame he would elicit after addressing the opening ceremonies of the World Trade Organisation (WTO) meeting in Seattle. He was, however, sadly disappointed. To get into the convention centre, Pettigrew had to be hauled by bodyguards and police over the flower pots to escape the demonstrators. When he arrived there was no one there to hear him—the opening ceremonies were cancelled when the trade ministers were unable to get to the doors. They were blocked by tens of thousands of demonstrators who had worked for months, organising buses, cars, trains and planes from across the US and internationally to ensure that the 'Millennium Round' meetings of the WTO did not go according to plan.

By the end of the meetings, on 3 December 1999, the WTO agenda was halted and ministers representing 135 countries left Seattle in disarray. The *New York Times* put it this way:

The collapse of the talks ended a tumultuous week of riots on the streets of Seattle, the arrest of more than 600 protesters and bitter infighting among 135 nations. They could not agree even on whether to discuss workers' rights and the environment in trade negotiations that were supposed to be started here. In the end, weary ministers headed for the airport without even issuing a final communiqué.[1]

What, then, was the agenda of the WTO Millennium Round summit meetings that provoked such a groundswell of opposition? What exactly did the successful protests at the Battle of Seattle achieve? What is the context of trade negotiations that have developed since the collapse of the Cold War? And what lies ahead in terms of building a movement that can effectively challenge a system driven by corporate greed? These are the questions that will be considered below.

Global trade agreements and capitalist crisis

Trade agreements are not new inventions. But since the collapse of the Stalinist state capitalist regimes the scramble for economic dominance among various blocs of capital in the world has intensified. The 1990s saw repeated rounds of negotiations for regional trade and investment deals. Huge multinationals, which dominate the world market, are intent on eliminating the state protections of weaker competitors. Most of these corporations are concentrated in North America and Western Europe. State support for less competitive national firms has been identified as a barrier to expansion for many years.

Now, however, efforts are being directed at formalising designated trade zones where tariffs and duties are virtually eliminated among the signing states, not only on industrial commodities but also on services and state welfare systems. In a drive to deregulation the largest, most competitive firms rise to the top, while the free market clears the less fit units of capital out of the way. But sections of capital that are threatened by a period of economic crisis turn to national states to bail them out, especially when their profit margins are so low that there is a threat of liquidation. The result is, in national economies, a lurching from policies of deregulation in periods of expansion to calls for state intervention in times of declining profits, as witnessed in South East Asia and Russia during the recent economic and financial crises.

Now there is a similar pattern on a global scale. When multinationals are in a strong position they push for an elimination of policies designed to protect foreign markets. This is the dynamic behind the drive in the WTO and the Free Trade Area of the Americas (FTAA) against local market subsidies, state support for weak industries or agriculture and the state regulation of services. If the prospects for economic expansion were to dim, however, which is inevitable in the capitalist system in the long run, these same multinationals would retreat to their home markets and call for state protections against foreign competitors. At the same time, economic arrangements do not exist in a political vacuum. Domestic political challenges have been critical in dictating the speed of implementation and degree of success in establishing international trade and investment deals.

The result is a drive to form international trade deals that raise the tariff walls to competitors outside the bloc but bring them down within the bloc's regional fortress. The WTO is distinct among international trade arrangements in that it incorporates a majority of the world's states. But the unevenness of the world system expresses itself inside the WTO, where the most developed countries attempt to assert their dominance over less developed countries. These deals are always unstable. They are alliances formed among international ruling classes that are by definition in competition with one another; the bosses are only ever temporary allies or, as Marx called them, hostile brothers. They unite to defend the family in a feud, but then return to endless squabbles over the inheritance. Such trade deals are also marked by contradictory pressures. They seek to establish market dominance for large corporate firms within an established trading zone, but they also represent international agreements among governments to drive down their home populations' standard of living. At the same time as profits increase, the deals subordinate every aspect of workers' lives to the rule of the market.

Some of these trade deals are, for a time, more successful than others. Despite massive internal disputes Europe has seen the establishment of a common currency, the euro.[2] The European Commission has recently recommended inviting six new countries to pursue full membership talks in the year 2000: Slovakia, Latvia, Lithuania, Bulgaria, Romania and Malta. Since March 1998 negotiations for full membership have been proceeding with Poland, Hungary, the Czech Republic, Slovenia, Estonia and Cyprus. Turkey has been proposed as a candidate for membership in the future. The imperialist designs that lie behind the extension of the reach of the European Union (EU) into the former Eastern Bloc and beyond is barely disguised. As Romano Prodi, president of the European Commission, announced to the European Parliament in mid-October 1999, 'Rarely in the course of history does an opportunity like this present itself. For the first time since the Roman Empire we have the opportunity to unite Europe'.[3] Similarly, despite some bitter trade disputes between the US and Canada over certain industries like fishing and lumber, these countries and Mexico have maintained the North American Free Trade Agreement (NAFTA) and are claiming resulting economic success.

Less successful efforts include the stalled negotiations to establish the Multilateral Agreement on Investment (MAI), comprising the 29 Organisation for Economic Co-operation and Development (OECD) states representing the world's largest economies.[4] Initiated by the US on the expectation of endless economic recovery, the return of crisis provoked protectionist policies among member states and fears of foreign competition. International disagreements and growing public opposition led to French withdrawal from the negotiations in October 1998, and the MAI died on the international order paper. However, part of the WTO Millennium Round agenda was aimed at resurrecting elements of the MAI in some form.

The Asia Pacific Economic Co-operation (APEC) group—an association of 18 economies including the NAFTA players, Australia, Indonesia, Japan, China and the once-mighty 'Asian Tigers'—first met in Canberra, Australia, in 1989. At the time the idea was to take advantage of the market miracle of Asian capitalism by establishing common conditions for trade and eliminating state controls. China was the newest and largest participant, with the most to gain in foreign investment opportunities and the most to lose through pressures to reduce state control of its domestic economy. A decade later APEC is adrift. Japan refuses to eliminate trade barriers that would open it up to the cheap goods of its now failing neighbours. Indonesia is in the throes of revolutionary upheaval. And the leader of 'Team Canada', prime minister Jean Chrétien, is haunted by scandal lingering from his ordering the use of pepper spray against anti-APEC demonstrators in Vancouver in 1997.[5]

The World Trade Organisation

The WTO was founded on 1 January 1995 with headquarters in Geneva.[6] As of March 1998 it comprised 135 member states, and China is now the most notable prospect to be the 136th. The WTO replaced the international trade agreement established 50 years ago, the General Agreement on Tariffs and Trade (GATT), which ended with the Uruguay Round (covering the last eight years of the GATT).

The WTO goes beyond the GATT, however, in that it covers not only industrial tariffs, but trade in many other areas—trade that affects the movement of commodities or the investment of multinational corporations. There are a series of regulations that member states of the WTO agree to accept. These trade rules include the General Agreement on Trade in Services (GATS), covering various services from refuse collection to education and healthcare; Trade Related Investment Measures (TRIMS), which relate to what governments are allowed to do in terms of regulating foreign investment; Canada and Japan are pushing for the measures of the failed MAI to be included under this agreement; Trade Related Intellectual Property Rights (TRIPS), covering rules on patents, copyrights and trademarks; in particular Canada and the US want to use this to advance corporate control of genetically modified foods; Sanitary and Phyto-sanitary Standards Agreement (SPS), which sets restrictive standards on government policies regarding food safety and animal and plant health; Financial Services Agreement (FSA), which is designed to remove all obstacles to financial services such as banks and insurance companies, and agreements on agriculture, information technology and telecommunications.[7]

The WTO also differs from any other global institution by having the ability to both legislate against particular practices and to act as judge to determine if those rules have been broken. This makes it an incredibly powerful tool for corporate interests. The rules of the WTO essentially define what areas of economic activity may be challenged as being a barrier to the development of the free movement of trade or investment by foreign corporations. The decisions regarding disputes are reached in secret by a panel of three unaccountable bureaucrats. Agencies outside of the governments and corporations directly involved—for instance environmental groups or labour unions—can only make submissions when they are endorsed by a government. One WTO official made clear the purpose of this process, and of the WTO more generally, stating,'The WTO is the place where governments collude in private against their domestic pressure groups. Allowing NGOs [non-governmental organisations] in could open the door to…all kinds of lobbyists opposed to free trade'.[8]

Regarding processes other than trade disputes, the WTO functions formally through a system governed by 'consensus'. But there is a group called the 'Quad' within the WTO comprising four key states, or actually groups of states, that meet daily to decide on how to address various issues. When the Quad comes to a conclusion they then declare that they have achieved 'consensus' to the other countries. The four members of the Quad are the US, the EU, Japan and Canada.

The WTO meeting in Seattle was intended to initiate the Millennium Round in world trade. The agenda for the Seattle meetings included three main areas: agriculture, intellectual property rights and services. Had the 'agriculture' agenda item been implemented, the plan was to ensure sweeping changes that define virtually all forms of farm subsidies as trade barriers:

*Small farmers could be wiped out because no small producer can compete with the heavily capital intensive, highly mechanised agriculture of Europe or the US, or even of the big **latifundia** in some of the Latin American countries. That means much more expensive food after wiping out the small peasantry.*

It would also mean vast outmigration to already overcrowded cities which would have totally catastrophic effects.[9]

Also on the table were proposed changes to the TRIPS agreement. These covered patents of such things as genetically modified organisms. Previous exemptions for Southern countries on agriculture and patents were now to be removed, allowing international corporations like Monsanto to legally control world markets in seeds for everything from flowers to grains. The US was also pushing for an agreement on wood products which would eliminate tariff and non-tariff barriers to importing or exporting forest products. This would allow major forestry giants to ignore environmental concerns to an even greater degree than they already do, and to use the WTO as a weapon to defend their practices.

One of the most profound changes in the politics of world trade is the formal redefinition of services as a trade barrier. The increasing privatisation of healthcare services in Canada and Britain has already provided a taste of things to come if supporters of free market policies have their way. The WTO agenda includes proposals to challenge state support for services which inhibit the flow of international capital. Services are defined by the WTO agenda to include the following: construction; wholesale and retail franchising; architecture; decoration; maintenance; civil, mechanical and other types of engineering; real estate; research and development; credit; communications, telecommunications and audio-visual services; information technologies; tourism and travel; sewage and refuse collection; water delivery; recreational, cultural and sports activities including libraries, archives and museums; publishing, printing and advertising; transportation of every type including space travel; corrections; and human and animal health.

Education is also included on the list. According to a document obtained by the Canadian Association of University Teachers (CAUT), US companies specialising in the export of private educational services—such as branch campuses, 'virtual education', and the international marketing of curricula and academic programs—gleaned US$7 billion in 1996 alone. This is the fifth largest service sector export in the US. 'Barriers' to further market expansion are now to be eliminated, according to the WTO, and such barriers include educational practices that inhibit 'innovation', and any form of subsidies for students, including bus passes.[10]

In case negative publicity is generated by such projects, the WTO defines itself as a trade organisation with a difference. Even before the Seattle summit there was clearly a concern among those responsible for the public relations of the WTO that its blatant commitment to facilitating greater profits for multinational corporations was too transparent. Instead we are expected to believe in the 'ten benefits' that the WTO claims to advance:

1) The system helps promote peace.
2) Disputes are handled constructively.
3) Rules make life easier for all.
4) Freer trade cuts the costs of living.
5) It provides more choice of products and qualities.
6) Trade raises incomes.
7) Trade stimulates economic growth.
8) The basic principles make life more efficient.
9) Governments are shielded from lobbying.
10) The system encourages good government.[11]

Furthermore, we are told that the WTO will promote world peace because:

Salespeople are usually reluctant to fight their customers... Two developments immediately after the Second World War helped to avoid a repeat of the pre-war trade tensions. In Europe, international co-operation developed in coal, and in iron and steel. Globally, the General Agreement on Tariffs and Trade (GATT) was created. Both have proved successful, so much so that they are now considerably expanded—one has become the European Union, the other the World Trade Organisation... What's more, smoothly-flowing trade also helps people all over the world become better off. People who are more prosperous and contented are also less likely to fight.[12]

The WTO is, clearly, not as united in its mission as its public relations propaganda claims. It is mainly Third World states that stand to lose, as trade disputes are settled in favour of the largest multinationals, concentrated in the US and the other advanced states represented by the Quad. Steven Shrybman, an expert on environmental law and global trade, and a leading Canadian critic of the WTO, summarises that 'notwithstanding a theoretical commitment to democratic practices, most developing countries consider the WTO agenda to be the exclusive domain of its wealthiest members'.[13]

India, for example, a regional power in its own right but low on the imperialist chain in the WTO, was at the centre of a dispute with the IMF that came before the WTO Appellate Body (the highest judicial appeal board in the WTO) in September 1999. The WTO ruled in favour of the IMF's claim that India's macroeconomic policies should be changed, as they restricted trade quantities in certain commodities in order to affect the country's balance of payments. In a decision celebrated by the US delegation and supported by the EU, a government's development policies were now identified as a barrier to free market forces.[14]

But even Canada has had its hand slapped. Canada has recently faced WTO rulings that challenge its favoured relationship with US car manufacturers, formalised in the 1965 Auto Pact, and the subsidising of the export of dairy products.[15] The US has also indicated that it plans to use the WTO to challenge the 'Canadian Wheat Board as well as Ottawa's 25 year old supply management systems for key agricultural products such as milk, chicken and eggs that have closed the door to all but a trickle of US exports'.[16] The thieves that met together in Seattle sat at the same table, but they were smiling through gritted teeth. The pre-existing fissures expanded into gaping cracks when a united opposition stood up against the WTO.

Behind the deals

In recent years there have been a flurry of high profile trade negotiations. These include trade and investment treaties like the MAI, free trade agreements such as the NAFTA, trade groups like APEC, and the consolidation of trading blocs such as the EU. Governments throughout the world have sought to expand international trade and exchange at the expense of the majority of their populations. The opening up of the global market, we have been told, is necessary to the advancement of economic prosperity. US president Bill Clinton responded to the signing of a trade deal between the US and China in November 1999, immediately prior to the Seattle meeting of the WTO, stating the following: 'In opening the economy of China, the agreement will create unprecedented opportunities for American farmers, workers and companies to compete successfully in China's market while bringing increased prosperity to the people of China'.[17] The trade agreement between the US and China was a precondition for the People's Republic to gain entry into the WTO. The deal, to be finally ratified in the US Congress, will see China's tariffs cut an average of 23 percent. It will also provide greater access for US banks, insurance companies, telecommunications firms, agricultural goods and Hollywood films to enter these previously closed sectors of China's economy. US companies will now have access to Chinese distribution networks, and auto companies will be allowed to offer vehicle financing.

US businessmen are drooling at the prospect of gaining entry into one of the world's fastest growing economies, with a potential consumer base of 1.2 billion people.[18] The Canadian government has pledged its intention to follow the US example and make a similar deal in order to get in on the profitable Chinese market. For the market reformers in China this deal and the hoped-for entry into the WTO will be used 'as a crowbar with which to open up China's economy'.[19] But this deal, like all the others, will not lead to the bread and roses that the world's leaders are promising. In China it will lead to huge increases in unemployment as state-run industries are forced into bankruptcy, adding to an already massive army of unemployed. In the US it will also undermine industries which cannot compete with the low wages of China's labour intensive industries, such as textiles.[20] The inclusion of China, despite its rhetorical political commitment to 'Communism', is in sharp contrast to the exclusion of Cuba from world trade negotiations. One of the largest trade deals currently under negotiation is the FTAA, a regional trade agreement launched by the US in 1994 and planned to come fully into effect in 2005. The US is the driving force behind the FTAA, but Canada is the other central player. Incorporating 800 million people, the FTAA will be the largest regional free trade agreement in the world. The FTAA includes 34 countries in North, Central and South America, and the Caribbean—all except Cuba. The exclusion of Cuba is on the grounds that only 'democratic states' are permitted access to the benefits of the FTAA. But countries like Colombia, El Salvador, Guatemala and Chile—which has only partly distanced itself from the brutal legacy of former dictator Augusto Pinochet—are upheld as models of democracy. The US insists that the democratic credentials of all other Latin American countries should not be under scrutiny. These so called democratic states have ruling classes that are, in some measure, literally trained by US governments. The School of the Americas at Fort Bening in Columbus, Georgia, has trained over 60,000 military and police personnel from Latin America in 'counter-insurgency'. One of the training manuals states that one way to enforce 'democracy' is to seek information from people by causing 'the arrest of the employee's parents, imprisonment of the employee or giving him a beating'.[21]

The pressures continue on sections of the world's ruling classes to establish a set of rules favouring the unfettered entry of the largest and most concentrated units of capital into larger world markets, and to access new sources of cheap labour. Today, despite soaring profits in the US and Canada, over the long term the prospects for the world economy continue to be unstable. In such a period large multinational corporations are forced to concentrate into larger and larger units that can be more competitive on a world scale. New trade initiatives are the expression of these economic factors. This was the background to the recent Millennium Round negotiations. The same driving forces are behind the move to extend NAFTA—which incorporates Canada, the US and Mexico—south, to become the FTAA. The FTAA is another focus of anti-capitalist sentiment on the American continent.

The Free Trade Area of the Americas

The FTAA is essentially a massive extension of NAFTA towards the south. The experiences of Mexico in NAFTA point to the future for other states in the region. NAFTA came into effect in 1994. It entrenched more than a decade of pro-market policies in Mexico, and eliminated remaining protections for small farmers and peasants. As a result, an estimated 1 million of these have been forced to abandon their lands through the 1990s. Many who can no longer live off the land migrate to Mexico's cities. A 1996 survey of Mexico's urban areas reported that 53 percent did not have enough food, 45 percent said they did not receive healthcare, and 29 percent stated that children age 16 or less had to work in order to support their families.[22] The collapse of the Mexican peso in 1994 led to recession conditions, but recovery came on the backs of the Mexican workers and peasants. By 1996, pro-free-trade US analysts were salivating over the expanded trade opportunities in the south.[23]

The FTAA is intended to incorporate and advance the trade relationships established through the Caribbean Basin Initiative and CARIBCAN, agreements that have promoted tax and duty free investment for US and Canadian capital.[24] Canada has a long tradition of defending, and benefiting from, US policy in the south (despite the formal contest over relations with Cuba).[25]

Negotiations to establish the FTAA are organised through nine 'working groups' with official names that indicate the scope of what's on the table. The groups are: market access; agriculture; investment services; government procurement; intellectual property rights; subsidies; anti-dumping and countervailing duties; competition policy; and dispute settlement. There are also three curiously grouped 'special committees'. These deal with 'smaller economies', 'experts on electronic commerce', and, most notably, the committee of 'government representatives on civil society participation'. 'Civil society', a term popularised amongst socialists by the Italian revolutionary Antonio Gramsci to refer to organisations outside the official state machinery, is now being touted by FTAA advocates. This committee is designed to attract input and consultation from groups like 'business' and 'labour'—as if these bear comparable influence—in a major international campaign to co-opt potential opposition. Rather than attempting to keep the deal secret, like the failed effort behind the MAI, or risking another Zapatista-style rebellion, like the one that welcomed NAFTA, the FTAA organisers are actively seeking to incorporate public criticism in advance.

However, like the WTO, the FTAA has not been proceeding without difficulties, even from other ruling classes. Brazil, for example, the world's ninth largest economy and producer of 45 percent of Latin America's total GDP,[26] is already in a trade alliance—called Mercosur—with Argentina, Uruguay and Paraguay. The FTAA has yet to establish how it will relate to Mercosur, and several smaller Latin American states are raising objections to the terms. And the pro-free-traders in the US have not been able to secure domestic 'fast track' legislation. Without it, any decisions of the FTAA can later be amended or reversed by the US Congress.

The opposition

This is the background to the explosive anger that erupted in Seattle in November and December 1999. Opposition to the WTO increased around the Seattle meeting in late November. Here is how the Seattle press covered plans for the protests:

> *The 30 November 1999 demonstration is 'likely to be the biggest protest in America against the globalisation of commerce'... Several activist groups see the Seattle meeting as the best opportunity to turn the tide of public sentiment against global free trade.*[27]

> *'It's historic...the confrontations in Seattle will define how the bridge to the 21st century will be built and who will be crossing it—transnational corporations or civil society.' That's Michael Dolan, field organiser for the Washington DC based Naderite group Public Citizen... Dolan is working on behalf of the Citizens' Trade Campaign (CTC)—a broad-based national coalition including Public Citizen; labour groups like the United Auto Workers; consumer groups; environmental groups like Friends of the Earth and Clean Water Action; farm groups like National Farmers Union and National Family and Farm Coalition; church organisations; and many more.*[28]

In the US, opposition from labour and environmental activists contributed to the stalling of 'fast track' approval in the Congress. In Europe awareness of, and opposition to, the WTO is rising.[29] In Britain a similar sentiment of opposition to corporate capitalism has been expressed in a campaign to cancel the massive debt burden of the poorest countries in the world. Third World debt has tripled from a 1982 figure of $700 billion to $2.3 trillion in 1999.[30]

An international movement that began in Latin America called Jubilee 2000 typifies the breadth of the opposition. This campaign is inspired by a Biblical reference to Jubilee, where every 50 years all debts were cancelled and slaves were freed. Beginning with a church campaign to make the year 2000 a Jubilee year, Jubilee 2000 has now won backing from labour unions and community groups throughout Latin America. In Britain Jubilee 2000 has gained support from labour bodies like the Trades Union Congress, the Transport and General Workers Union, the UNISON public sector union (the largest union in Britain), and the Fire Brigades Union.[31]

Before the demonstration against the WTO this sentiment was expressed in a demand for an immediate moratorium on the Millennium Round of the WTO. This demand was endorsed by 1,100 signing organisations in 85 different countries.[32] The particular political terrain in each country is key to the level and character of organised opposition. The US opposition is obviously central. This is not only because of the pivotal role of US capital and the US state in the WTO, the FTAA and world trade in general, but also because the Millennium Round of the WTO was launched, and stalled, in a US city.

The US labour federation, the AFL-CIO, called for the demonstration in Seattle, but it did not demand that the WTO be stopped. Instead the AFL-CIO was 'strictly calling for the incorporation of workers' rights agreements into the WTO'.[33] Some US union affiliates refused even to endorse this demand. Tragically, their leaderships tied their organisations to the US Democratic Party, which is certainly no friend of US labour or the rights of the poor.[34] Sections of the trade union bureaucracy—the minority layer of full time officials who are far removed from the interests of the rank and file—are nervous about embarrassing Al Gore, US vice-president and a pro free trade Democratic presidential candidate, in a pre-election year.

It is in this context—that of an effort to reform, rather than stop, corporate trade agreements—that the Committee on Civil Society of the FTAA has attracted dozens of contributions from organisations, including labour unions, in virtually every one of the prospective member states. The extent of the involvement is impressive in reflecting the mood of the times—ranging from high school class submissions to neighbourhood church group letters to labour federation policy documents from Canada, the US, Mexico, and Central and South America. Some have detailed arguments about why the FTAA should be stopped. But the leading voice of opposition to the FTAA is expressed in the Hemispheric Social Alliance formed in May 1997 in protest against the FTAA Ministerial Meeting held in Brazil. In their final statement, the Alliance announced that their goal was to fight for 'fair trade' through the inclusion of the labour and environmental civil society organisations on the same scale as business and government.

Take the example of Canada. There is an established history of angry opposition to international free trade arrangements like the WTO and the FTAA. A mass coalition of forces, led primarily by the social democratic New Democratic Party (NDP), and the major labour federations and trade unions, but also including organisations like the Council of Canadians, Citizens Concerned About Free Trade (CCAFT), and numerous academics and public figures, has opposed the implementation of the Free Trade Agreement (FTA—a deal that combined Canada and the US in a trade deal that preceded NAFTA), NAFTA and the MAI.

There is a gap between the anger against these deals at the base of society and the leadership of the opposition movement. It is a gap that has been characteristic of anti-free-trade campaigns for some years. What is significant about the terrain of struggle since the Battle of Seattle, however, is that in that pivotal confrontation the anger from below went far beyond the demands of the leadership that had called the protest. This has opened new arguments on the ideological front.[35]

In the current round of trade debates two things have changed in terms of the dominant arguments on the left. And these changes are more significant after the events of Seattle. First, the corporate interests in these trade deals have now become much more transparent. Serious critics of corporate power are looking for a persuasive explanation of what is happening in the world system. Susan George, for example, a leading international trade analyst and virulent opponent of the WTO, has concluded:

> *The only explanation seems to be, as Marx and Engels put it, that 'modern state power is merely the executive committee charged with managing the affairs of the bourgeoisie'. This 'bourgeoisie', now embodied in huge transnational industrial and financial corporations, makes itself heard loud and clear by 'state power' via multiple lobbies. Among these, the International Chamber of Commerce (ICC) has a special place, claiming as it does to be 'the only representative body that speaks with authority on behalf of enterprises from all sectors in every part of the world'. It makes its demands known directly to heads of state.[36]*

The ideological terrain is incredibly favourable to Marxist explanations. However, the flow of ideas is not going only in one direction. At the same time as conscious opposition to the rule of capitalism as a system is growing, the political forces best situated to challenge this, the trade union leaderships and the labour parties internationally, are caving in to the market.

The second change in the current round of trade debates is the Blairite turn of other social democratic parties. The NDP's position on NAFTA is a case in point. Rather than calling for its elimination, the NDP now calls for the removal of the investor-state mechanism which allows corporations to directly sue governments which 'unfairly' restrict trade. Similarly with the WTO and the FTAA: the NDP, rather than calling for their abolition, seeks 'enforceable international rules on core labour standards, environmental protection, cultural diversity, the preservation of public healthcare and public education, and, generally, the right of democratically elected governments to act for the common good'.[37] However, quality labour standards mean higher wages and investment in health and safety conditions, which directly cut into profit maximisation. Environmental protection requires support for indigenous peoples' agricultural land rights and regulations on multinational agribusiness. Protecting the environment, again, means cutting into profits and giving way to the competition. But profits are the *raison d'être* of the WTO and the FTAA.

The NDP has taken its admiration for market mechanisms on a domestic level, which mimic the policies of Tony Blair, to the international level. Now, rather than opposing the domination of the world market by multinational corporations, the NDP is fostering the illusory position that the world capitalist market can be repaired, reformed, to meet the needs of workers and the poor. This shift in the NDP's orientation also reflects a shift in the Canadian Labour Congress (CLC), which represents 2.5 million unionised workers. Like the AFL-CIO, there is a gap between the trade union officials who lead the CLC and the interests of rank and file workers who comprise the vast majority of its membership. The CLC leadership's submission to the Committee on Civil Society of the FTAA indicates the same objective, to repair rather than oppose the FTAA.[38]

So while reformist ideologies face a crisis, it is not inevitable that working class internationalism will benefit. Instead, trade union and NDP leaderships have moved from a defence of national capitalism against 'foreign ownership' to a call to repair the international market in a type of international Blairism. However, to call upon these organisations, and others like them, to reform and address the demands of workers and the poor is like asking a leopard to change its spots. The WTO and the FTAA are institutions of international capitalism, designed to further that system at the expense of the majority of the population on the planet. They cannot be made nicer or more gentle. The FTAA should be stopped in its tracks before it goes into effect in 2005. And the WTO should be shut down. This is the sentiment of the majority of protesters who won the Battle of Seattle, but it is not the objective of the leadership of the anti-free-trade movement.

What next?

The failure of the MAI in 1998 made governments nervous about pushing through the new agenda in world trade. After Seattle this nervousness has been replaced by confusion and disarray. In addition the delegates from the Third World countries found their confidence to oppose the Quad agenda boosted by the demonstrators. Here is how *The Toronto Star* attempted to 'begin the autopsy of what went wrong':

The Europeans refused to move on export subsidies and the Americans refused to move on anti-dumping issues. But perhaps most significantly for the future of the World Trade Organisation...the less developed countries making up the majority of the group refused to be ignored any longer. Despite a last ditch effort in the form of a 14 hour, closed door meeting to hammer out a final declaration to launch a new round of trade talks, the negotiations fell apart late Friday night... While 30 of the largest countries were invited to Friday's all-important meeting, delegates from Third World countries were left to mill about in nearby souvenir and coffee shops... Delegates from Third World countries credited protests in the streets during the four days of negotiations for producing the resolve to fight to be heard at the talks, even if it meant scuttling the negotiations. 'The people who demonstrated basically represent the silent majority,' said Papua New Guinea trade secretary Michael Maue.[39]

Meanwhile across the US, and in Canada, Europe, Latin America and the Caribbean, there are groups of activists meeting and planning how to keep up the momentum against corporate control. The covers of all the major news magazines had to recognise that a new era had come to pass. The lead article in *Newsweek* in the 13 December 1999 issue was 'The Battle Of Seattle: The New Face Of Protest. Is The WTO Good For America?' *Time* magazine opened the same week's edition with 'Trading Blows: Will Seattle's Days Of Rage Change The Face Of Global Capitalism?' Pressure from rank and file activists on the trade union leaders and social democratic parties to organise and lead the anti-market activists will increase, at the same time as the ideological commitment to the market from the leaderships of these organisations remains.

On the other side, the ruling class agenda on world trade is in disarray. At their 17 December 1999 General Council meeting the WTO officials could only agree that they would not make any decisions. A post-Seattle statement indicates the success of the protests in paralysing the world's most powerful trade organisation:

The WTO General Council on 17 December 1999 decided to postpone until early 2000 a decision on how to proceed with issues outstanding from the Seattle Ministerial Conference. One group of proposals on the table at the Seattle Conference sought delays in end of year deadlines for applying obligations and other provisions of WTO agreements—for example in intellectual property (TRIPS) and certain investment measures (TRIMS). Members could not agree on whether to accept or reject the delays, or to consider them individually member by member. These deadlines will now be among the subjects discussed in consultations in the new year, and members agreed in the 17 December General Council meeting to exercise restraint and understanding in dealing with the deadlines while the consultations are under way.[40]

There is no unified plan about how to proceed in the WTO, and the pro-free-trade pundits are bitter. *The Economist* chastised the 'non-governmental organisations and their swarms', but was forced to admit that the NGOs 'were a model of everything the trade negotiators were not. They were well organised. They built unusual coalitions (environmentalists and labour groups, for instance, bridged old gulfs to jeer the WTO together). They had a clear agenda—to derail the talks. And they were masterly users of the media'.[41]

Our side won the battle, but the war is still on. The logic of the system will compel more attacks. As corporations become larger, they seek out markets and cheap labour and resources in every corner of the world. Governments try to help out local capitalists by prying open foreign economies. In their endless search for greater profits, human needs, the environment and basic services are all treated as barriers to profits which must be removed.

One of the oldest examples of the effects of this system is the border zone in northern Mexico, where the *maquiladora* factories, mostly US-owned, have been running with virtually no restrictions on trade or investment since the program was initiated in 1965. The *maquiladora* zone was a model for NAFTA, and NAFTA is the current model for the FTAA. With over 30 years experience, the *maquiladora* zone is like a human laboratory, an example of what will become generalised across the globe if the forces behind the WTO and the FTAA have their way.

The free trade zone is one of the most profitable in the world, and its profits are directly related to how little the companies spend on wages or working conditions. So while handling PCBs, or polychlorinated biphenals, is banned in US factories because of its known links to cancer, the same corporations can use PCBs liberally on the Mexican side of the border, though this will not be admitted when cases are heard in court. The mothers of the 'Mallory Children' washed the capacitors—tiny television parts which store an electrical charge—in a liquid they called 'electrolito'. Their fingernails turned black and they were always very tired at the end of their shifts. When they became pregnant they hid this from their bosses for fear of being fired. Then they saw their babies born with brain damage and webbed feet.[42]

This is only one story. There are hundreds more—the victims of the world market far outnumber those who profit from it. But workers and the poor are not only victims. There is today a very widespread sentiment of opposition to the dominance of multinational corporations over the world system. When APEC leaders met in Vancouver in 1997 the brutal dictator of Indonesia, President Suharto, was wined and dined as Canada's guest while protesters outside were beaten and pepper-sprayed by police. The workers and students of Indonesia sent an inspiring message around the world when they toppled Suharto in a mass revolution in 1998 and began a process of transformation that continues to this day. Building a revolutionary alternative to a system bent on corporate greed is now the order of the day.

Notes

1   J Kahn and D E Sanger, 'Seattle Talks On Trade End With Stinging Blow To US', *Sunday New York Times*, 5 December 1999, p1.
2   For background on this see A Callinicos, 'Europe: The Mounting Crisis', *International Socialism* 75 (Summer 1997).
3   'EU Seeks Six New Members: Powerful Bloc's Numbers Would Nearly Double', *The Toronto Star*, 14 October 1999, pD9.
4   P Kellogg and S Whitney, *The MAI and Capitalist Crisis: A Marxist Analysis* (International Socialists, Canada, 1998).
5   J Armstrong, R Matas and D LaBlanc, 'New Tapes Raise Questions About PM, APEC: Senior RCMP Officers Appeared To Believe Chrétien Had Direct Say In Security', *The Globe and Mail*, 23 October 1999, pA4.
6   S George, 'Trading Places', *Socialist Review* 233 (September 1999), pp18-19.
7   M Barlow and T Clarke (Council of Canadians), 'A WTO Primer: An Activists' Guide to the World Trade Organization', p1 (http://www.canadians.org/campaigns-tradepub001.html).
8   Council of Canadians, 'WTO Backgrounder', p1 (http://www.canadians.org/campaigns-tradepub02.html).
9   S George, 'Trading Places', *Socialist Review* 233, op cit, p18.
10   'New Trade Rules Target Education', CAUT Bulletin, vol 46, no 7 (September 1999), p7.
11   'Introducing the World Trade Organisation', http://www.wto.org/wto/10ben/10ben00.htm
12   Ibid.
13   S Shrybman, *The World Trade Organisation: A Citizen's Guide* (Canadian Centre for Policy Alternatives and James Lorimer and Co, 1999), p3.
14   M Khor, 'Appellate Body Decision on India's Balance of Payments Erodes Developing Countries' Right to Make Macroeconomic Policies', Third World Network SUNS 4515, 24 September 1999, South-North Development Monitor SUNS E-mail Edition, Penung, Malaysia (mkhor@igc.apc.org).
15   J Deverell, 'Dairy-Industry Subsidy On Exports Ruled Illegal'; and T Van Alphen 'Tariff Changes Ordered To Historic Auto Pact', *The Toronto Star*, 14 October 1999, ppD1, D8.
16   'WTO Targets Subsidies To Farmers', *The National Post*, 13 October 1999.
17   S Holland, 'Clinton Hails US-China Market Opening Deal', Reuters, 15 November 1999.
18   'China Deal To Boost Economy', BBC News, 15 November 1999 (http://news.bbc.co.uk/hi/english/business/the_economy/newsid_520000/520874.stm)
19   T Karon, 'Clinton Lobs A Hail Mary Over China Trade Deal', *Times Daily*, 2 November 1999 (http://www.pathfinder.com/time/daily/0,2960,33568-101991102,00.html).
20   Ibid.
21   K Dwyer, 'School of the Assassins', *International Socialist Review* 9 (Fall 1999), p26.

22 L Selfa, 'Mexico After the Zapatista Uprising', *International Socialism* 75 (Summer 1997).

23 J P Sweeney, 'Restoring American Leadership in Latin America', *The Heritage Foundation Backgrounder,* No 1092, 25 September 1996.

24 See A Bakan, D Cox and C Leys (eds), *Imperial Power and Regional Trade: The Caribbean Basin Initiative* (Wilfrid Laurier University Press, 1993).

25 'Canada's Export Performance Closely Linked To US Economy, Study Shows', *International Trade Reporter*, vol 13, no 17, 1 May 1996, pp723-724, cited in J P Sweeney, op cit.

26 *The Observer*, 4 October 1998, cited in A Callinicos, 'World Capitalism at the Abyss', *International Socialism* 82 (Winter 1998), p10.

27 *Seattle Times*, 10 September 1999.

28 *Seattle Weekly*, 8 August 1999.

29 S George, op cit, pp18-19.

30 M O'Brien, in 'Debt Crisis: Who Pays?', *Socialist Review* 223, op cit, p14.

31 J Hanlon, in 'Debt Crisis: Who Pays?', *Socialist Review* 223, op cit, p15.

32 A Cash, 'What Canucks Are Doing', *Now Magazine*, 21-27 October 1999, p25.

33 G Parrish, 'Yankee Unions Pull Plug On Own Protest', *Now Magazine*, 21-27 October 1999, p25.

34 A Cohen, 'Gore Campaign Gets Bounce From Backing Of Big Labour', *The Globe and Mail*, 15 October 1999, pA19.

35 The left nationalist position, which dominates the leadership of the movement in Canada, has called for anti-free-trade workers and students to ally with sections of the Canadian ruling class in opposition to 'American domination'. Exactly where this logic can lead was demonstrated by the entry of CCAFT leader David Orchard into the leadership race of the federal Conservative Party in 1998. It is clear that the interests of students, workers, the poor and the oppressed do not lie in joining with the Tories. Yet some 7,000 activists joined the Tories during the leadership campaign as a result of Orchard's call, and, in the context of a massive vacuum of Tory leadership, he came in a remarkable second place to the front line winner, former premier Joe Clark. This is the same party which brought us the FTA and NAFTA. This is the party of the hated former prime minister Brian Mulroney and the 1990-1991 Gulf War.

36 S George, 'Globalising Designs For The WTO: State Sovereignty Under Threat', *Le Monde diplomatique,* July 1999 (http://www.tni.org/george/wto/lemonde.htm).

37 'NDP Opposition Day Motion', 4 November 1999, http://caucus-ndp.ndp.ca/reports/wto/default.asp?/load=motion

38 D Martin, 'Presentation to the Round Table on the Free Trade Area of the Americas (FTAA)', 13 April 1999, http://www.clc-ctc.ca/policy/trade/ftaa.html

39 S Laidlaw, 'World Trade Group Calls Timeout', *The Toronto Star*, 6 December 1999, pA13.

40 'General Council Defers Post-Seattle Discussion Until Early 2000', http://www.wto.org/wto/new/gc_seat.htm

41 'Citizens' Groups: The Non-Governmental Order', *The Economist*, 11-16 December 1999, pp3, 20.

42 This example is drawn from A Dwyer, *On the Line: Life on the US-Mexican Border* (Latin American Bureau, 1994), pp66-67.

In perspective: Susan George

MARK O'BRIEN

Join in any debate or discussion about hunger, world poverty and the effect of world capitalism on the poorest countries, and at some point the name of Susan George will be mentioned. George is an example of a rare breed. She is one of those independent scholar-activists who for 25 years has written and campaigned against the horrors of the global system, neither being deflected by often vicious attacks from the establishment nor by the flatteries of academia. From her earliest published works through to her latest writings, what shines through is a passionate anger at the inequities of a system that condemns hundreds of millions of human beings to lives of brute survival, and at the hypocrisies of those who benefit from that very state of affairs. It would be wrong to call her a 'development theorist' or an 'economist' in the normal sense. Rather, she is a champion in the cause of social and economic justice. As she says of herself:

> I have always sought to understand and to describe how power is deployed. From this vantage point I have dealt with such subjects as world hunger and Third World poverty, the impact of southern hemisphere debt, North-South relations, transnational corporations and institutions like the World Bank.[1]

An American settled in France, she is currently the associate director of the Transnational Institute based in Amsterdam—a loose coalition of radical academics working for social change. She has also served on the board of Greenpeace International (1990-1996), and is associated with the left wing French publication *Le Monde diplomatique* and with campaigns such as Jubilee 2000, which has led the movement for the abolition of Third World debt. This list of credentials could go on, but it will suffice.

George has rightly been a highly influential figure. With the growth of an increasingly radicalised consciousness in both the advanced industrial countries and in the less developed countries around issues of world trade, the misuse of science and ecological ruin, the audience for her writings has also grown. She urged us on to action against the World Trade Organisation at the end of 1999 and many of the protesters at Seattle must have been familiar with her work.

In her first book, *How the Other Half Dies* (1976), she uncompromisingly exposed the way in which capitalism destroys the lives of the poorest people on our planet. Her essential aim in the book is to explain world poverty not as a terrible but unavoidable phenomenon, but rather as something which flows from the logic of the system itself. More than this, George draws out the deliberate manner in which the inequalities of the system are maintained. She does this in a number of ways. She demolishes attempts by apologists for the system to explain away poverty as a thing unconnected with the normal workings of capitalism. She looks at the political and social mechanisms by which the wealthy elites of the poorer countries are brought into the fold of the West. George also argues that technological 'solutions' in and of themselves, imposed with no regard for local economies and cultures, bring misery to those who are pushed aside by such developments. Finally, she looks at the workings of the large 'agribusiness' corporations and the politics of food aid.

The first thing George does, however, is to hit the reader with the facts of the problem at that time. It should be borne in mind that by the time George was writing her book in the mid-1970s the road of national development for most of the hitherto 'developing' world had hit bumpy ground. The capitalist post-war boom was long since over, and the world economy was in deep crisis. It was around this time that Third World countries were first beginning to move towards the International Monetary Fund (IMF) and the World Bank for lending to finance their development programmes. The first IMF-inspired austerity measures were soon to be introduced in countries as far apart as Egypt and Jamaica. This was the historical moment when the seeds of the crippling debt burden of the southern hemisphere that we see today were being sown. What George is describing in her book—though it may not have been obvious to most at the time—is the experience of economic *reversal* for the populations of the Third World. The facts about, and the scale of, the problem were staggering (and are worse today):

>...in the Asian, African and Latin American countries where well over 500
>million people are living in what the World Bank has called 'absolute
>poverty'.[2]

At the time this meant that these human beings were struggling to live
on about 30 cents a day. In some areas, George explains, half of all children could be expected to die before the age of five, and worldwide more
than a fifth of all children were malnourished. One in every eight people
were literally starving, and half of the world's population were suffering
from malnutrition of one form or another.[3] In the Third World a child was
15 times more likely to die before its first birthday than in the West.
Indeed, infant mortality rates in such countries were similar to those in
Europe around 1750. She examines also the diseases of the poor: goitre,
affecting 300 million; pellagra, caused by a monotonous corn diet; beri-
beri, caused by iron deficiency; blindness, caused by vitamin A
deficiency; the parasitic diseases—malaria, yellow fever, bilharzia. All
of them both avoidable and treatable given the right social conditions
and medical support, but all of them blighting the lives of hundreds of
millions of the poorest in the world. To complete the list today we would
need to add tuberculosis, HIV/AIDS, cholera, dengue fever and many
others which have either appeared since George wrote her pathbreaking
book, or which have reappeared from having been pushed to the margins
by medical advance and the social improvements of the 1960s.

After having given a picture of the scale of the human suffering
involved, George now turned to the causes of the problem. This was
nothing to do, she argued, with 'natural' disasters. As she points out,
'drought, which is a frequent occurrence in the south western United
States, is not at all the same thing as drought in the Sahel'.[4] Neither, as
some had started to argue following the apocalyptic predictions of Paul
Erhlich, was the problem caused by 'overpopulation'. When we consider
just how influential this pernicious idea was to become, not just on the
right but also on the left and within the Green movement in the 1980s,
George's clarity on the question is impressive. As she points out, there is
no correlation whatsoever between the population density of a country
and the levels of hunger in that country:

>...famine exists both in Bolivia, with five inhabitants per square kilometre,
>and in India, with 172—but there is no famine in Holland, where there are
>326.[5]

As she insists, it is not large family size that leads to poverty, but rather poverty that creates the economic need for children:

> *Another baby for a poor family means an extra mouth to feed—a very marginal difference. But by the time that child is four or five years old it will make important contributions to the whole family—fetching water from the distant well, taking meals to father and brother in the field, feeding animals ... children are an economic **necessity** for the poor.*[6]

Another issue on which George stood out against the crowd was that of the 'Green Revolution'. This phrase was bandied about in the mid-1970s by the popular press to refer to the new strains of high yield crops (HYCs) that had been developed by American bio-scientists working for the Rockefeller Foundation in Mexico. These 'miracle' crops would, it was claimed, eliminate hunger and famine once and for all. The reality, however, was that these crops were often vulnerable to local plant diseases and lacked the necessary background genes for hardiness in coping with local climatic conditions. The deals that farmers had to enter into to obtain these HYCs stipulated that they also had to import expensive fertilisers produced by US agribusiness companies when much cheaper, locally manufactured fertilisers were available. But much more fundamental than all of these was the fact that the destination of these new crops was never going to be the poor who needed them most. Rather, the produce of this modern agricultural revolution was bound for world, and particularly Western, markets. It was the export orientation of Third World economies that was ultimately to take food from the mouths of the hungry. The result was that whilst rice production in India rose dramatically, rice consumption actually fell. It was the system then, George argued, that had to change:

> *...given a different social system and a concerted effort to make the new technology benefit all the people, the revolution can be just what it was touted to be—a road towards self sufficiency and the eradication of hunger. It need not be a poisoned gift.*[7]

George, however, reserved her greatest scorn for the major political and economic institutions of the West. She pointed out the way in which food and 'food aid' had become a weapon of political and economic power in the world. She cited the examples, amongst many, of the refusal of food aid to Chile during the period of the Popular Unity government under Allende, and the cutting off of food aid to the newly independent countries of Cambodia, Laos and Vietnam after the US's military defeat there in 1974.

The CIA meanwhile announces...that increasing grain shortages could give 'Washington...virtual life and death power over the fate of the multitudes of the needy'. This is exactly what food has become: a source of profits; a tool of economic and political control; a means of insuring effective domination over the world at large, and especially over 'the wretched of the earth'.[8]

In the 1980s Susan George focused her attention on the structural mechanisms which tied Third World economies into such an unfavourable relationship with the rest of the world economy. With characteristic perspicacity she homed in on an issue which has today become a focus for mobilisation around the globe—that of Third World debt. In her 1988 book, *A Fate Worse Than Debt,* George charted the effect of IMF and World Bank intervention in the poor countries and the ravages of the structural adjustment policies they imposed.

The huge borrowings granted by the major lenders in this period were not for social or welfare spending. The spin-offs of increased investment into housing, health and education which had come with the industrial development of the 1960s were already a faded memory. An unholy alliance had emerged between the IMF, the World Bank and local rulers in which economic coherence had been put to one side. George describes the way in which the highest bids for the building of sugar refineries, for example, would win because of the large margin for palm-greasing which had been included in them. Vast building projects with little strategic purpose were undertaken. She cites the example of the Morong (Batan) nuclear power station commissioned by president Ferdinand Marcos of the Philippines at a cost of $2.1 billion. The plant was inoperable because it had been built on an area of high volcanic activity—but it did contribute handsomely to the personal fortunes of the Marcos family! This was the era of the 'white elephants'.

Another area for which loans were forthcoming was that of military spending. By 1982 Third World spending on arms stood at over £12 billion:

It is precisely the poorest countries, especially those in Africa with large debts to service, that tend to spend most heavily on national security... The end result for the 1972-1982 decade...is that 'the value of arms transferred to the non-oil developing countries more than doubled in real terms between 1972 and 1982, and their share of total world arms transfers increased from 31 percent to 41 percent in the same period'. Not surprisingly, this was precisely the period during which the debt burden was accumulating.[9]

In most of the rest of the book George surveys the damage and human cost of the effects of IMF-imposed conditions in large areas of the Third World and the early impact of the structural adjustment policies. In

Africa the effects of IMF policies could be seen at their most extreme—and this is still the case today. In terms of world trade Africa was at best marginal, accounting for only 4 percent of the total. With the IMF financial regime coming on top of this the result would be crippling. As George commented:

> *This doctrine is now creating perverse effects beyond anything imaginable a few years ago. IMF rigidity may bring ruin to an entire continent, and for years to come.*[10]

She was right. Even when she was writing in the late 1980s, all of the classic indices of living standards were worsening and swinging towards the extremes. When the Kenyan government carried out its Rural Child Nutrition Survey in 1982 it found that 28 percent of children under five were stunted compared to 24 percent ten years previously. It also revealed chronic sickliness in nearly half of all children. In Zaire real wages had fallen to a tenth of what they had been at independence and 80 percent of people were living in absolute poverty.

> *Malnutrition has been on the rise since 1983; cases of kwashiokor (the swollen belly syndrome) are way up; in some regions 'people say half the children are now dying before they reach the age of five'. One survey shows that in the two biggest cities—Kinsasha, the capital, and Lubumbashi—the average daily calory rations are 1,450 and 1,425. According to the Food and Agriculture Organisation, the daily caloric intake needed for a reasonably active life is 2,300; levels in Zaire are thus indicative of slow starvation.*[11]

It was George's unique contribution at this time to also link the issue of Third World debt to that of ecological destruction as concerns about the environment were entering mainstream debate. For George at this time the issue was primarily the way in which major building projects, undertaken with little regard for long term ecological consequences, affected the lives of people within particular countries. The impact of such things as the removal of topsoil, the diverting of rivers, the 'cashing in' of natural resources to service debts and the forced transmigration of millions of indigenous people are all examined. She also discusses the effects of rainforest clearance and highlights the loss of thousands of plant species of unknown and untapped potential. Today we are also aware of these issues as things that are affecting the planet as a whole.

The Debt Boomerang (1992) was a collaborative work undertaken with others from the Transnational Institute, but for which George assumed overall responsibility. The book explores the ways in which the burden of Third World debt affects the economies and societies of the

West. In places it also provides a welcome antidote to the notion that workers in the West benefit in any sense from the exploitation of the populations of the poor countries.

Continuing her theme of the environmental consequences of the exploitation of the Third World, George illustrates the link between debt and deforestation:

> *Of the 24 largest debtors, eight never had or no longer have forest reserves significant on a world scale. Of the 16 remaining major debtors...all are found to be on the list of major deforesters. The correlation is particularly strong for mega-debtors such as Brazil, India, Indonesia, Mexico and Nigeria, all of which rank among the top ten deforesters.*[12]

To heavily indebted countries such as these the rainforests are either a source of revenue in themselves in terms of the hardwood exports, or they need to be cleared to make way for the grazing of cattle or the growing of modern cash crops. The fact that rainforest clearance is a major contributory factor to global warming is not a serious concern to the capitalist companies caught up in the rush for short term profit. If the ruthlessness of the companies involved in the destruction of the rainforests needed any further illustration we should remember the murder of Chico Mendes, who organised the rubber tappers of Brazil in an attempt to harmonise their need for a livelihood with the need to maintain the rainforest itself.

George also charts the impact of the debt crisis on jobs in the West. As consumption levels have fallen in Latin America, for example, so markets for goods from the US have also contracted. In 1983 the *Quarterly Review* of the Federal Reserve Bank had noted a drop in exports to Latin America which would lead to a loss of a quarter of a million jobs in the US. In fact, by the following year the US had 560,000 fewer jobs caused by the loss of exports since 1980. George extrapolates that a further 800,000 jobs would have been created if the growth of the 1970s had continued after 1980.

> *Thus nearly 1.4 million jobs have been lost due to the recent recession in the Third World. Adding up the losses each year since 1980 the poor performance of US exports to the developing countries has cost a total of 3.2 million person years of employment—an average 8.4 percent of official unemployment during the period.*[13]

Another sense in which workers in the West have paid for the debt crisis is the way in which Western banks have transferred the costs and risks of lending onto taxpayers and ordinary depositors. The major creditor banks protect themselves against losses in a myriad of ways. One is by tax relief on 'non-performing' loans. George gives figures which show that the UK Inland Revenue was set bear about $7 billion of the $20 billion of outstanding loans at that time. Other losses were spread over long periods of time and incorporated into bank charges.

We can conclude from all of the above that workers in the West, far from having gained from the exploitation of the Third World, have directly lost out because of the instabilities and unevenness the debt has produced. Whilst the banks have achieved hitherto undreamt of rates of return on their lending in the Third World, workers in the West have paid. On the other hand, however, there is a hint here of one of George's more problematic themes. This is the notion that there is a conflict of interest between finance and productive capital within which an appeal to the 'rational' side of the system can be made. We will return to this after looking at her most recent work, *The Lugano Report*.

The Lugano Report (1999) is an ironic and polemical book. George writes as though she is the voice of a 'working party' commissioned by the governments of the advanced capitalist world to examine the question of what the main threats are to the capitalist system, and what measures must be taken to preserve capitalism in the next century. The picture which George paints does capture something of the gloom which hangs over any speculation about the future of capitalism today. Overall, however, the result is a mosaic of some important insights, a whiff of conspiracy theory and more than the occasional flight of fancy.

George begins by pointing up the great contradiction of capitalism identified by Marx 150 years ago—that on the one hand capitalism is the most productive system in history so far, and yet has created the most extreme wealth alongside the greatest extremes of human misery. As George says, the world now produces the equivalent of the entire physical output of the year 1900 in less than two weeks. Despite this, the prognosis of the 'working party' for the future of the system is grim. Ecological breakdown is likely, they argue, in the foreseeable future. Global warming and freak weather patterns will reach a critical, irreversible stage and will have a catastrophic impact on human life. Economic development will be distorted by increasingly negative and irrational features. 'Gangster' capitalism will run rife in large parts of the world. Drug barons and arms dealers operating outside of any regulation, or national or international law, will become increasingly powerful. The corruption of government officials will become the norm. Financial meltdown, they continue, despite their unshakeable faith in the free market, is an ever-present danger. These oracles of the system also achieve the insight that class struggle may just be a problem for them in the future.

Sharp social divisions and 'class struggle', as Marxists perhaps still call it, constitute a genuine menace. Beyond a certain threshold, disparities are dangerous for the system and must be carefully monitored.[14]

The apocalyptic conclusions of the report, they argue, can only be avoided with some measure of regulation. Excesses of competitive behaviour between multinational companies must be curtailed, as well as the dangers of 'pernicious growth' leading to overproduction and collapse. The national state must play no role in this. That would be counter to the very principles of the free market. Rather, they suggest, some of the institutions of global capitalism may play such a regulatory role. The World Trade Organisation, they suggest, is a 'promising candidate for international success' in this area.

The 'working party' are especially concerned, not to say obsessed, with the 'problem' of population. The system, they argue, cannot support present levels of population growth. The world has polarised, they argue, into a one third/two thirds division in which the third that is better off has a stake in terms of wealth, security, careers, jobs etc and in which the other two thirds are in effect shut out of the world system. The conclusion reached is that the liberal democratic societies of the West are only sustainable for a third of humanity. The 'working party' now 'unflinchingly' reaches its most shocking conclusion—that the other two thirds of humanity must go. By 'go', the 'authors' mean literally just that—that they must be eliminated. They are not, they demur, proposing a Holocaust-type final solution. There will be no opprobrium here. Rather, population reduction will be achieved through both preventative and curative measures. Preventative measures will reduce the birth rate. The removal of reproductive freedom will play a part in a new 'biopolitics'. The mentalities of the 20th century must be changed and a transvaluation must occur.

Biopower and biopolitics must henceforward focus not on vitality but on mortality, promote not reproduction but reduction, seek not longevity but brevity. The task is historical, philosophical, even metaphysical in scope. The mentality which has dominated the West for two centuries must be transformed; it must become the obverse, the opposite of its former self. It must understand and welcome the necessity of death and seek to prevent life.[15]

As you try to catch your breath, the 'authors' press on. Curative measures, dealing with those people already born, will mean a positive fostering of the great scourges of humanity. Warfare and inter-ethnic conflict will be encouraged through the selling of ever cheaper arms and political destabilisation. Famine will play its role as a 'population curb', as will increasingly limited access to land and drinking water. Pestilence and the diseases of poverty will also do their work. Food aid will end and the market will cut off those unable to buy. The historical Enlightenment project to improve the lot of all mankind will end. The experts who make up this working party are vicious Malthusians.

Now, all of this does conjure up the sense of deep pessimism and despair felt by many who see no alternative to the present system. It also rams home the chilling reality of the horrors that capitalism is quite capable of delivering. However, George is not just being dramatic here. She does suggest that such thinking is indeed going on in powerful circles in the advanced countries, and that she would not be in the least surprised if such a document had indeed been produced by a similar working party.

It is often difficult in the *The Lugano Report* to pick out where George is saying what she actually thinks and where she is imagining how such a working party might think. This makes a critical appreciation of the argument she is putting forward problematic. What is clear, however, is that she does believe that capitalists—or at least powerful sections of the capitalist class—are able, actually or potentially, to exert a high degree of control over their system. Even the premise of this level of collaboration between the advanced capitalist powers glosses over the intense rivalries between them which make their alliances unstable. Most recently we can point the tensions within the World Trade Organisation (WTO) between the US government and European governments over the issue of banana imports into Europe. This was one well-publicised instance of the much larger issue of genetically modified produce and the desire of US biotech companies to break into lucrative European markets with this new generation of foodstuffs. Indeed, the fiasco of the Seattle WTO conference in November 1999 and the failure of the represented governments to reach agreement on trade can hardly have inspired confidence amongst the major capitalist powers in their ability to regulate their system, even in their own terms.

A constant theme running through all of George's work is the notion that the barbarities of the system she has so brilliantly charted are to do with the *mal*development of capitalism. The problem then becomes one of how world capitalism is managed, or rather *mis*managed. For George, the enormous increase in the activity of the financial sector is a key distorting factor in the world economy. The influence of finance capital, then, is seen as a *cause* of the warped priorities of the system rather than as being one of the *effects* of the long period of capitalist crisis which neatly covers the period over which George has been most active and influential. The qualitative growth of the banking sector and the activity of finance capital has it roots in the period of low profit rates and stagnation of the 1970s. Large firms which could not afford the cost of capital investment to update plant and machinery to compete on world markets chose instead to speculate with profits on the major money markets of the world. The financial and manufacturing sectors of world capitalism, then, are two interpenetrating sides of the of the same system. There is no 'more rational' side to the world system representing the potential for 'development'. George does not recognise this sufficiently.

The weakness of George's analysis of the economic roots of the crisis of world capitalism leads directly to an uncertainty as to who her audience actually is. Often her writings read as an appeal to opinion formers and practitioners within government or development circles. This is very much the case in *A Fate Worse Than Debt.* In the '3-D' (debt, development and democracy) solution she proposes that a combination of enlightened repayment policies linked to strategic investment and controlled import-export schemes with the West would begin to inch Third World countries back onto the path of development. Again there is the appeal to the interest of one section of capitalism (manufacturing) over another (banking). This is a kind of alternative economic strategy for the Third World. There is also some of this in *The Lugano Report,* where she puts forward the Tobin tax—a proposed tax of about half a percent on all foreign exchange earnings—as a way of controlling the excesses of the money markets whilst generating revenue for Third World investment. This is reformism at the level of international financial markets. In her most recent comments on the significance of the Seattle protests, her proposals border on an almost utopian belief in the humanitarian good sense of some elements within capitalist governments:

> *Suppose the ILO and the United Nations Enviroment Programme were to classify all countries at a given level of development—including the most advanced—according to the respect they show for labour law and for nature. The best, at each level, would be granted tariff preferences or even exemption from customs duties, while the produce of the others would be taxed according to their classification.*[16]

It is this belief in a section of capitalism to which progressives can appeal that leads George to a 'management' solution to the problem. But why, she wonders, has the ideology of the free market become so strong in the last decade? With no real notion of the organic crisis of the 1970s grounding her analysis, she concludes that it must have been the result of a purely ideological guerrilla campaign waged by the free market right over this period:

> *Why have we not learned from the single-mindedness of the right? Why can we not see, for example, that the destruction of welfare in the United States or*

the threats to trade union achievements in Europe would have been impossible without the creation of an intellectual climate making such onslaughts appear not morally repugnant but natural and inevitable?[17]

What is needed, she says, is a similar project from the side of those who seek change for the better. This project, she argues, must move beyond 'left and right'. What she means by this is that some sections of capitalism may be won to the humanitarian side:

Sometimes the allies, in a truly bizarre twist, may even be...transnationals. The insurance industry, for example, is exceedingly worried about global warming because it increases the frequency of tropical storms. One needn't agree on everything to agree to work on something, although I draw the line at major predators and polluters.[18]

This strategy would be a long term one of changing the intellectual consensus within the circles that matter. Funders of research in development circles and non-governmental organisations should back the work of researchers in these fields, George argues. The strategy here is one of laying intellectual siege to the system in order to pave the way for a new enlightenment in international relations. This is a direct appeal to progressive academics.

But George is vacillating. On the one hand she is concerned with looking for levers of influence within the development agencies. On the other she is aware of the self limiting nature of such an endeavour and looks instead to activism. This is where she is at her best. All of her books have the admirably non-academic distinction of ending with the question, 'What can we do?' Indeed, there are passages in her books which read as a call to arms:

...the burden 'we' must shoulder in the coming century is nothing less than the intervention of international democracy. The alternative is totalitarianism and the Lugano Report: the choice is between their rulers and ours.

We are in a similar position to that of the Americans or the French in the mid-18th century... I don't know if our century is more mature, if we can invent non-violent solutions and succeed without bloodshed—I hope so—but I know that this is not the end of history and that we must try to put down transnational tyranny before it puts us down. Like our ancestors, we must move from subjecthood to citizenship, from being victims to being actors in our own destiny.[19]

There is a revolutionary sentiment here, but for George the 'we' is unclear. The agents of radical change for her include everybody from grassroots activists involved in community campaigns, consumer boycotts and consciousness raising, to those involved in civil society initiatives such as workers' self help organisations and co-operatives, development agencies and non-governmental organisations, trade unions, those involved in government, and even some transnationals. George is a writer concerned with the question of power, but she does not locate a social force which is adequate to the task of challenging the power of capitalism itself. There is no sense in George's writings of the revolutionary potential of the working classes of the Third World and of the West.

In the end, this is the most serious shortcoming in George's perspective. Strong on exposing the problems but weak on the question of political strategy, George sees no *essential* role for the working class in any transformation of the world economic order. In fact, in every part of the world where the effects of IMF austerity measures have been felt, workers have resisted. From the anti-IMF riots against Sadat's government in Egypt in the 1970s onwards, the impositions of the World Bank and the IMF have produced urban riots, strike movements and insurgency. However, it is not just the role of the working classes of the Third World with which we should be concerned, but also that of the Western working class.

In her discussion of Seattle in the January issue of *Le Monde diplomatique*, George does talk about the involvement of the AFL-CIO and the organising role these unions played that day. For George, however, this is merely one element in a wide and complex coalition of forces. George misses the most exciting and important fact—that 40,000 US workers (Teamsters, steel workers, etc) joined forces with the Seattle protesters and in doing so reached out the authentic hand of working class internationalism to their brothers and sisters in the oppressed countries of the world. It is such actions and their reciprocation that the new world consciousness manifested at Seattle will fuse with the rise of different national working classes around the world to prepare the ground for international solidarity and revolution.

Despite the critical remarks made here it would be churlish to end on a negative. George has done important work, and many people have been radicalised by the way in which she has brought home the true scale of the barbarity of modern capitalism. After three decades of radical scholarship and campaigning she remains an optimist for the struggle ahead:

> If you're fatalistic you say that capitalism just rolls on like a juggernaut, crushing greater parts of humanity and the environment. But the system is fragile, with lots of cracks. We just have to get out there with our pickaxes and work along the faultlines. I've sometimes been criticised for my pessimism, but I must say I'm as optimistic now as I have been in a very long time. I really think there are huge opportunities now.[20]

Notes

1   S George, *The Lugano Report* (Pluto, 1999), p189.
2   S George, *How the Other Half Dies* (Penguin, 1986), p23.
3   Ibid, p31.
4   Ibid, p44.
5   Ibid, p58.
6   Ibid, p59.
7   Ibid, p130.
8   Ibid, p16.
9   S George, *A Fate Worse Than Debt* (Penguin, 1989), pp23-24.
10 Ibid, p87.
11 Ibid, 108.
12 S George et al, *The Debt Boomerang* (Pluto, 1992), p10.
13 Ibid, p97.
14 S George, *The Lugano Report*, op cit, p9.
15 Ibid, p92
16 *Le Monde diplomatique,* January 2000.
17 S George, 'How to Win the War of Ideas: Lessons from the Gramscian Right', *Dissent* 44:3 (Summer 1997).
18 S George, *The Lugano Report*, op cit, p184.
19 Ibid, p184.
20 Interview in *New Internationalist* 320 (January-February 2000).

Chechnya: the empire strikes back

ROB FERGUSON

—What is this place called?
—'Valerik', said he,
Which means 'The river of the dead'
And those who named it rest in Heaven.
—How many did the Mountaineers lose?
—Who knows? Why would they be counted!
'They'll be counted', I heard a voice reply
'This day of blood will not be forgotten'.
I turned and saw the Chechen, nodding,
With a grin of contempt upon his lips.
Mikhail Lermontov, 'Valerik', 1840[1]

On 31 December 1994 young Russian conscripts in tanks and armoured personnel carriers advanced into the bombed ruin of the Chechen capital, Grozny. Many had hardly left their schoolrooms. They came from Rostov in the south; from Vladivostok on the Pacific; from the Urals; from Moscow and St Petersburg; from the Arctic north. They came from small provincial towns and from the great, decaying, broken spirited industrial heartlands of Russia. The column passed down Pervomaiskoye Street towards the presidential palace, and towards the units of Chechen streetfighters lying in wait amongst the ruined apartment blocks.

Armour piercing, rocket propelled grenade launchers were fired at point blank range as the Chechen snipers and light machine gunners pinned the terrified soldiers down inside their vehicles. Grenades were dropped from balconies. View ports were covered with tarpaulins. Those who clambered from their ambushed vehicles fell alongside the shattered tank tracks and the burning armour that served as crematoria for those still trapped inside. As Russia celebrated the new year hundreds of young men lay dying in agony and terror in the Caucasus.[2]

Official death counts were adjusted to avoid political embarrassment to the generals and the politicians in Moscow, but back in their home towns the broken bodies added a fierce and bitter fuel to Russia's internal discontent. Over the succeeding months Russia's military pounded the Chechen forces back to the southern mountains. But the body count rose inexorably and Russia's desertion-ridden conscript army never recovered its morale. In the summer of 1996 the Chechens retook the capital, having swept a despairing, unpaid, ill equipped military force, once the pride of the world's second superpower, to what seemed its final humiliation. Two hundred years after the tsars first set out to conquer the 'Mountaineers' of Chechnya, their victories had turned to dust.

But now, hardly six years on, the Chechens again face the horror of war, military occupation and slaughter. Again their lands have become the crucible for Russian domination over the Caucasus. And once again the 'new world order' steps bravely into the bloody footprints of the old.

The Caucasus: imperialism and conquest

The states that make up the Caucasus today were forged on the anvil of Russian imperialism. The Caucasus literally means 'the mountains', and it spans the territory between the Black Sea and the Caspian. To the north lies Russia, to the south Turkey and Iran. It extends across Russia's path to the Black Sea and to the Bosphorus, Russia's sea route to the Mediterranean. Here the tsars' imperial ambitions clashed with those of Persia and the Ottoman Empire, and Russia embarked on a massive campaign of conquest, determined to secure the 'great barrier' on its borders and its route to the sea. The peoples of the Caucasus paid the price.

The territories of the region contained a multiplicity of peoples and, in order to divide and undermine its potential foes, Russia deliberately fostered deep ethnic and religious rivalries. Whole peoples were put to the sword. During the 1860s a million Cherkess and Turkic Caucasians were butchered or driven into exile. Circassia, on the eastern shore of the Black Sea, ceased to exist. The Abkhaz population fell by more than half. The Caucasus became the empire's chessboard upon which hundreds of thousands of lives were ruthlessly expended.[3]

Russian rule in the Caucasus was part of an age of 19th century imperial conquest by the Great Powers. It looms large in the writings of

Pushkin, Lermontov and Tolstoy, represented in language reminiscent of Kipling and the British Raj. But the people who stride most often across their pages are those who rose in the greatest of the Caucasian revolts against the tsars—the Chechens.

Chechnya: the crucible of revolt

> The Russians...assign religious fanaticism as the primary cause of this and all similar outbreaks; but in truth it is only secondary. It was in the role of invaders, oppressors, conquerors—or, to use the current euphemism, civilisers—that they excited such bitter resentment... The Ghazavat [holy war] would never have been preached in the Caucasus had the Russians been peaceful and friendly neighbours.[4]

Until the 19th century the Chechens were largely isolated from the encroachments of settlement and the incursions of passing armies, protected by the mountains and great forests. Even their language had a unique root, shared only with their cousins, the Ingush. Like mountain peoples elsewhere, their social structure reflected their sparse surroundings. Family groups maintained themselves more or less independently, relying on their own crops, pastures and livestock. The Chechens enjoyed a relatively equal status compared to the sea of serfdom to their north, but were often divided by the need to safeguard their means of economic survival, and they manifested an obsessive demarcation of possessions and holdings.[5] These divisions were reflected in bitter rivalries and blood feuds.

Yet the Russian invader threatened all. Forests were cleared, crops burned, villages destroyed. Forts were constructed and tsarist law imposed. Resistance was met with the most savage slaughter. General Yermelov urged his commanders to 'destroy *auls* [villages], hang hostages, and slaughter women and children'.[6] As one Russian officer chillingly observed, 'Our actions in the Caucasus are reminiscent of all the miseries of the original conquest of America by the Spanish'.[7]

The Chechen revolt of the 19th century is therefore one of the most remarkable instances of resistance in modern history. It inspired the opponents of reaction across Europe, including Marx, who sang the praises of its foremost leader, Imam Shamil. The wars lasted half a century, costing Russia tens of thousands of lives. At their height 200,000 tsarist troops were engaged. In 1845, in just one of many Russian defeats, Vorontsov's 10,000-strong army was forced to flee, having lost three generals and 3,628 men.[8]

The key figure in this resistance was Imam Shamil, an Avar from

Daghestan. He united the disparate settlements, clans and tribes under the banner of his Sufi brotherhood, the Nakshabandi.[9] The Nakshabandi preached equality between rich and poor, and combined the aspiration for spiritual reformation with that of liberty from oppression. But Sufiism not only provided spiritual inspiration, it transformed the mountain peoples' social organisation. In order to enable mobilisation on a scale sufficient to face the Russian armies, Shamil had to establish a structure of rule and unite the mountain peoples under one command. His Sufi brotherhood combined both religious and military organisation through the *murids*, or disciples. These charismatic religio-military commanders and administrators established a system of military rule over the heads of local chieftains. At the heart of their nascent state lay a new structure of common law, *sharia*. The petty rivalries between families, villages and clans were now subjected to superior authority as *sharia* became a tool in the struggle against Russian oppression. As John F Baddeley observes, 'The new teaching was essentially popular, and from this time onward Muridism was a political movement grafted upon one in itself purely religious'.[10]

Shamil and his commanders were able to gather and disperse their armies at phenomenal speed against the Russians. When one Russian general thought he had thrown his enemy into flight, 10,000 Chechens appeared to attack another. Shamil fought the Russians for a quarter of a century, but his defiance could not last. The Russian onslaught combined terror and slaughter on an unprecedented scale and served to undermine the very basis of Shamil's new social institutions from within. They razed the vast forests with fire. Villages were destroyed and their inhabitants massacred. Every family suffered. Tens of thousands were driven north. A vast swathe of land was effectively depopulated. Grand duke Mikhail Nikolayevich explained, with the impeccable logic of the imperialist butcher, 'It was necessary to exterminate half the Mountaineers to compel the other half to lay down its arms'.[11] The Russians broke the allegiance of local chieftains to Shamil with pardons and pensions, and the unity that he had forged began to tear asunder.

The material basis for Muridism lay in military mobilisation. As the Chechens recoiled under the Russian onslaught that basis began to disintegrate. The exactions of the Sufi military administrators were increasingly resented. As Shamil became besieged, he resorted to ever harsher methods. Where inspiration failed terror was deployed, leading to ever greater demoralisation and collapse.

In 1859 Shamil finally surrendered. Over 25 years 70,000 Chechens had died, one third of the population. Shamil continues to inspire the Chechen fighters today but it was not his aim, nor was it within his ability, to establish a Chechen nation. Baddeley astutely observes that the conceptions of the mountain peoples were 'still limited for the most part to the narrow bounds of the communities into which from time immemorial they had been divided'.[12] This, however, was to change. And it changed under the hammer blows of revolution and dark reaction.

New dawn, dark night: from Red October to the gulag

Muslims of Russia! Tatars of the Volga and the Crimea! Kyrgys and Sarts of Siberia and of Turkestan! Turks and Tatars of Trans-Caucasus! Chechens and mountain people of the Caucasus! All you whose mosques and prayer houses used to be destroyed, and whose beliefs and customs were trodden underfoot by the tsars and oppressors of Russia! From today your beliefs and your customs and your national and cultural constitutions are free and inviolate. Organise your national life freely and without hindrance... Comrades! Brothers! Let us march towards an honest and democratic peace. On our banners is inscribed the freedom of oppressed peoples.

Thus read the 'Appeal to All Muslims, Toilers of Russia and the East', issued by the Council of People's Commissars, 3 December 1917. It was the banner of revolution that at last created the possibility of breaking the tsarist yoke. In 1919 the north Caucasus rose in support of the Bolsheviks and tied down one third of General Denikin's White Army. In March 1920 Grozny fell and Deniken was evacuated by the British. But local rulers feared the threat to their own power. With the White armies defeated, the imam Najmudin Gotsinski led a rising against the Bolsheviks in September 1920. Their attitude was expressed by Gotsinski's predecessor, Ujun Haji: 'I am weaving a rope to hang engineers, students, and in general all those who write from left to right' (ie in Latin or Cyrillic script).[13] Many Chechens and Ingush fought solidly alongside the Bolsheviks against Gotsinski, led by the outstanding Caucasian revolutionary Najmuddin Samursky.[14]

Finally, in 1921, a Mountainous Autonomous Republic was created and a constitution granted based on *sharia* law.[15] Chechen and Ingush artefacts stolen by the tsars were returned, as were the lands occupied by Cossacks who had fought with Denikin. The Chechens had no written language, so a new Latin script was devised and for the first time books and newspapers were published written in Chechen. Literacy rates soared. For the first time in their history a free nation was being forged from the fires of revolution. The possibility of liberation and fraternity began to open up across the Caucasus.

However, the window of freedom began to close all too prematurely. Stalin's chauvinism and divisive manoeuvres as Commissar for

Nationalities were already beginning to leave their dark stain. And worse was to come. At the end of the 1920s the last vestiges of the October Revolution were swept aside. In 1929 tens of thousands of troops were deployed in the Caucasus to crush a rebellion in eastern Chechnya and quell disturbances over 'collectivisation' of land. The Chechen historian Abdurakhman Avtorkhanov recounts how, in 1930, the regional party secretary, Chernoglaz, an ethnic Russian, mounted a wave of repression across Ingushetia. In the village of Galashki an old man, imprisoned for assassinating the tsarist governor no less, stood to address him:

> *I was sentenced to penal servitude for life, but 12 years later the revolution liberated me. The Soviet government is good, but you, Chernoglaz, are a bad man. I do not want to kill you. Instead, I am giving you wise advice: go away from Ingushetia while you still have a head on your shoulders.*[16]

Chernoglaz had the 'old bandit' arrested. That night Chernoglaz was killed and beheaded.

The Chechen revolt against Stalin was unique for the leading role played by Chechen communists, 'Old Bolsheviks' who had fought Ujun Haji in 1921. Stalin wreaked a terrible vengeance. On one night in 1937 14,000 Chechens and Ingush were rounded up and killed in mass executions and buried in a common grave at the base of Goryachevodskaya mountain. The massacre triggered yet another rebellion, brutally crushed. Stalin's purges now spread their pall over the Caucasus. Countless numbers perished in the gulag.[17]

In 1944 Stalin perpetrated the greatest crime in the history of the mountain peoples of the north Caucasus. In his bloody determination to crush any possibility of nationalist resistance emerging in the aftermath of war, the entire Chechen and Ingush population of half a million were deported to Kazakhstan along with the Kalmyks, Karachais, Balkars, Meskhetian Turks, Crimean Tatars, Pontic Greeks, Kurds and Koreans. Over 130,000 Chechens and Ingush died. The operation diverted 100,000 soldiers, 12,000 train carriages and fleets of Studebakker lorries from the front. Four thousand oil workers were deported. At the village of Khaibakh the Russian secret police, the NKVD, ordered 700 people who were too old or weak to walk down from the mountains to be burned alive in a barn.[18]

The deportations are the defining moment of the modern Chechen experience. Street names were changed and gravestones uprooted to pave the roads. A statue of General Yermelov, the favourite butcher of the tsars, was erected in Grozny, bearing the inscription, 'There is no people under the sun more vile and deceitful than this one.' Every Chechen over 60 can remember the deportations. A generation of

Chechens were born in exile.

In 1957 the then Soviet president, Khrushchev, gave the Chechens permission to return and granted them their former territory.[19] This was not just benevolence on his part. In exile the Chechens had forged a new unity in the face of suffering and hardship. They organised work strikes and a mass breakout of 4,000 at Krasnoyarsk in Siberia. Secretly, increasing numbers left Kazakhstan for Chechnya, braving arrest and imprisonment. By 1957 it had become impossible for the authorities to stem the flow. The character of the Chechens' experience had been transformed. The separateness of mountain and rural life had been broken by the experience of deportation and exile. Their social unity was further deepened by economic development. Between 1959 and 1989 the Chechens rose from 9 percent to 42 percent of the urban population.[20]

But the ordinary Chechen always remained a second class citizen. Public discussion of the deportations was prohibited until 1989. On every key socio-economic indicator Chechnya, despite its oil wealth, ranked bottom of all the regions of the Soviet Union. Ethnic Russians dominated the top posts in the party and state apparatus as well as industry. Russians received preferential allocation of housing. Young Chechens faced unemployment and were forced to rely on seasonal labour in construction and on collective farms outside Chechnya.

In 1991 the Chechens watched the world's second superpower collapse. For the first time in 70 years the prospect of freedom once more raised its head. But the 'new world order' that appeared to promise so much was soon to turn into an era of renewed imperialist rivalry. It was in such circumstances that Chechnya embarked on its struggle for independence.

The politics of oil and the fuel of war

Russia is participating in this confrontation between world powers in disadvantageous conditions. But in spite of this, we must defend our position on the Caucasian bridgehead. **Kim Tsagolov, Russian Deputy Minister for Federation and Nationality Issues**

The Caspian oil supplies and the pipelines that criss-cross the region are a vital factor in the rivalries between the regional powers in the Caucasus and the major imperialist powers. The importance of oil lies not only in its commercial value, but in its strategic significance. An oilfield is a fact of geography. You either control the tap or you do not. Military blocs and alliances become as important as commercial contracts. Britain, the Ottoman Empire and tsarist Russia all vied for the Caucasian oilfields, which became a crucial objective for the German army during the Second World War.[21]

The collapse of the Soviet Union and the formation of newly independent states along its borders has now paved the way for a return of what in the 19th century was called 'the Great Game'. Under the shadow of the major imperialist powers, regional states vie to control both the supplies and the pipelines. Ethnic and nationalist conflicts become weapons in the battles for regional dominance. There is not a single state not subject to these explosive tensions. Since 1991 there has been an almost permanent state of conflict across the Caucasus. Georgia has suffered a civil war and two separatist conflicts in Abkhazia and South Ossetia. During 1992-1993 Armenian troops, bolstered by Russia, fought Azerbaijan over the Armenian enclave of Nagorno-Karabakh. When this war threatened to extend to the Azeri enclave of Nakhichivan, Turkey threatened to bomb the Armenian capital, Yerevan. The Russian republic of Ingushetia clashed with neighbouring North Ossetia. Turkey is fighting an ongoing war against the Kurds. Chechnya is now suffering its second invasion. To the south lies Iran, whilst across the Caspian lies Central Asia, itself a site of war and conflict.

War	Dead	Refugees
Ingushetia-North Ossetia, 1992	750	65,000
Georgia-South Ossetia, 1990-1992	1,800	100,000
Georgia-Abkhazia, 1992-1993	40,000	250,000
Georgia—civil war, 1992-1993	300	—
Armenia-Azerbaijan, 1992-1994 (Nagorno-Karabakh)	30,000	1,000,000
1st Chechen war, 1994-1996	40,000-80,000	350,000
2nd Chechen war, Sept 1999-	10,000*-.........	220,000
TOTAL CASUALTIES	122,850-162,850	1,985,000

* Estimates are almost impossible to judge but this must be a minimum figure

Russia has continually intervened in these conflicts in its bloody determination to reassert dominance over its 'near abroad'. NATO for its part is making strenuous efforts to draw key states into its own sphere of influence, expanding along the whole of Russia's southern flank. The formation of GUUAM, the NATO-inclined bloc consisting of Georgia, Ukraine, Uzbekistan, Azerbaijan and Moldova, is one evident example. Azerbaijan has even called for NATO to protect the planned Baku-Ceyhan pipeline. This route, one of the key options amongst several backed by the US, would pass from Azerbaijan through Georgia and eastern Turkey to the port of Ceyhan.[22] Considering the geography of conflict outlined above the latest James Bond plot, aptly titled *The World is Not Enough*, has the appearance of a mild disturbance in comparison to this explosive mix of regional rivalries and imperialist interference.

Whilst Russia could not prevent the 'union' republics from breaking away in 1991, it has gone to great lengths to reassert its power and influence through economic pressure and by fomenting conflict and division, backed by the threat of its own military force. An independent Chechnya would represent a massive blow. If Chechnya (a country smaller than Wales) was victorious, Russia's strategy for the Caucasus and the whole of its 'near abroad' would be in jeopardy. And much as the US and NATO would like to see Russia weakened in respect of their own military and economic might, a Chechen victory would also represent a blow to imperialism as a whole, sending a signal to the oppressed across the region that they too could defy the great powers and win.

The phoenix rises: independence and war

In 1947 Tony Cliff wrote:

> *The struggle for national independence against Russian imperialism is sure to continue as long as Russian imperialism does. It is one of the most important factors which could seal the fate of the Stalinist regime.*[23]

The collapse of the Soviet Union was indeed heralded by the growth of mass independence movements across the former Soviet republics. From the Baltic states to Central Asia, millions took to the streets to demand an end to decades of dictatorship and oppression. A new future, full of hope and liberty, seemed to beckon. 'Popular fronts' were formed to demand greater autonomy, democracy and, finally, independence. As the Soviet power structure shook, erstwhile Communist leaders were faced with the choice of trying to ride the storm by recasting themselves as nationalists, or throwing their lot in with the old regime. The turning point came with a vengeance. In August 1991, a group of hardliners launched a putsch in Moscow and declared a state of emergency. A key objective was the annulment of a new Union Treaty granting the republics greater autonomy and the prospect of independence. Either the putsch would be defeated or the hopes of the popular movements would turn to ash. The coup failed, and the Soviet Empire went into melt-down.[24]

When news broke of the *putsch* in Chechnya, vast crowds poured in from the villages and towns to fill the centre of Grozny. In the midst of a general strike Doku Zavgayev, the Chechen party boss of 15 years standing, was dragged out of a sitting of the Supreme Soviet by the crowd and forced to sign an 'act of abdication'.[25] A new leadership took power, demanding full independence, led by general Dhokar Dudayev and the Congress of the Chechen People.

The congress had been formed in 1990. The founders included moderate figures from the elite and some adventurists, all looking to carve out a new role for themselves from the ruins. The first congress was organised by the head of the state road construction company and bankrolled by the oilman Yaragi Mamodayev. A key figure was Beslan Gantemirov, former policeman turned racketeer, now turned Russian stooge. They rode with popular sentiment, demanding greater autonomy and democracy.

The key figure, however, was Dudayev. He had resigned his commission and returned to Chechnya with the aim of turning the congress into a radical political movement for full independence. Dudayev was no Islamic rebel from the hills. He was 'a model Soviet officer'. He had commanded a bomber fleet in Afghanistan, destroying the mountain villages that gave support to the *mujahaddin*. In 1988 he was promoted to command a division of long range strategic nuclear bombers in Estonia. He had bitter memories of exile, but had been educated in the Soviet Union and had spent very little of his life in Chechnya. As Lieven noted, he appeared 'uncomfortable in his new Chechen skin'.[26]

Dudayev won 85 percent of the vote in the presidential elections in October 1991. In November he declared Chechnya an independent republic. Moscow's response was to send in the notorious Interior Ministry police. This was met with fury by a population that had returned the highest vote in the whole of Russia for Yeltsin in the presidential elections five months before.[27] Hundreds of thousands turned out to demonstrate in Grozny, and Moscow was forced to pull back. Dudayev's position was now secured and Chechnya became a *de facto* independent state.

However, Chechnya's position was precarious, caught between the collapse of the command economy on the one hand and a world market too ailing to regenerate some forgotten corner of the Caucasus. The Chechen leaders' pleas for recognition went studiously unheard. Not one state thought that the much vaunted new world order of independent nations extended to the Chechens. Here the line in the sand was finally drawn.

The new Chechen leadership degenerated rapidly, following in the footsteps of the ruling class across Russia itself. Any assets that could be seized and converted to cash were carved up between them, often with the aid of armed criminal groups. As ordinary Chechens saw the very fabric of modern life fall apart, the Chechen rich were ever more prominent. In this the ruling class in Chechnya was no different to that of Russia itself. The image of the Chechen 'bandit' comes rich from Moscow politicians accustomed to carrying sports bags with hundreds of thousands of dollars in 'campaign contributions', and whose foreign bank accounts are awash with nice fat chunks of an estimated $60 billion of capital that has 'flown' the country.[28] But the impact of the corruption and growing misery upon the Chechens was evident.

By 1994 Dudayev and his regime had become deeply unpopular. The Kremlin was optimistic that they could deal with their errant republic. Dudayev was despised and the regime seemed shaky. Russia cut the oil supplies and the economy went into free fall. Vladimir Zhirinovsky's fascist Liberal Democratic Party had rocked the Kremlin with a massive rise in electoral support during the December 1993 elections to the Russian parliament. Yeltsin's advisers saw bringing Chechnya to heel as an opportunity to restore the president's standing. In addition, as the jockeying over the oil pipeline routes from the Caspian gathered pace, Russia faced the problem that the cheapest pipeline option ran through Chechnya. Moscow backed and armed a stooge Provisional Council set up by opponents to Dudayev which launched an 'attack' on Grozny supported by Russian units. It proved a fiasco and in the face of a humiliating rout the pressure built for direct armed intervention by the Russian army. The stage was set for war.

The shelling of Grozny that began in December 1994 marked the heaviest artillery bombardment since the Second World War. At the height of the siege of Sarajevo 3,500 shells a day fell upon the city. In Grozny it was 4,000 an *hour*.[29] The foundations were destroyed and water supplies and sewerage systems demolished. And as Anatol Lieven points out:

Grozny was not some small, half-baked provincial town of the Third World; it was a large industrial city, the second biggest oil refining centre of the world's largest oil producing country, and formerly the world's second biggest industrial power. The oil refineries around Grozny are themselves whole cities, stretching for dozens of square miles.[30]

The majority of victims in Grozny were ethnic Russians. Two thirds of the city's population had been Russian and unlike many Chechen inhabitants they had no relatives in the villages to whom they could flee. An estimated 27,000 civilians died in Grozny alone, predominantly the old and poor.

Outside Grozny Chechen civilians were herded into 'filtration camps' as suspected 'bandits'. Many were thrown into mud pits or subjected to electric shock treatment. Rape and summary executions were widespread.[31] Red Cross vehicles were shelled and reporters shot. The tsars' brutality had returned to Chechnya with all the armoury of modern warfare.

Popular resistance and the ghost of Imam Shamil

You could say that the whole population is involved in the defence. Every street has provided several groups of four or five volunteers... If they see something suspicious, they fire three shots, and all the armed men in the town will take up position...behind us there is a local staff, made up of men with Soviet military experience... There are no formal commanders here. We just work together... As you see we are not an army. We are just ordinary people defending our homes.[32]

The myths of Russian propaganda regarding the character of the armed Chechen revolt have permeated out to the West. The foremost is that of the Chechen 'bandit formations', the terminology used by Russian imperialism for two centuries. The second is that of Islamic fundamentalist terrorists, linked to that pantheon of villains which stretches from Osama bin Laden to Gadaffi.

The Russian army was not defeated by 'bandits', but by popular resistance. Here the role of two emergent military commanders, Shamil Basayev and Aslan Maskhadov, is especially significant, representing two strands of military and political leadership. Maskhadov was Dudayev's chief of staff. As a colonel in the Soviet army he had served all over the USSR and Eastern Europe. Shamil Basayev described his own childhood as that of 'an all-Soviet kid'. He had studied in Moscow and there found inspiration from Che Guevara (whose picture he kept in his pocket throughout the war). During the 1991 *putsch* he stood on the steps of the Russian parliament to defend Yeltsin. His military experience came as a fighter in the Abkhaz war against Georgia in 1992-1993 and he draws on the image of Imam Shamil to provide a historical root for his modern version of Islamism and for a vision of a united mountain people of the north Caucasus.

Both commanders were instrumental to the defeat of the Russians in the 1994-1996 war and they demonstrated a fantastic grasp of both guerrilla and urban warfare. But the war was not won simply by virtue of guerrilla armies made up of mountain villagers and the unemployed young men who had grown up during the Soviet collapse. There was another element: spontaneous uprisings by large numbers of ordinary Chechens, many of whom were workers from Grozny and other towns. Lieven describes watching a column of volunteers in the ruins of Grozny, 'marching towards the roar of the guns, into a battle against apparently hopeless odds, cheering as they went: 'One old man raised his fist and cried, "No pasaran!"—the kind of soldiers of whom most commanders can only dream'.[33] The war became a combination of classic guerrilla war and spontaneous popular militias. It was this, combined with the low morale of unpaid Russian conscripts who were treated as sheer cannon fodder by their commanders, that created the conditions for the Russian defeat.[34]

However, the dynamic of war exposed deep rooted political tensions within the Chechen leadership. In mid-1995 the situation was desperate. The guerrillas were under siege in the southern mountains and their mountain villages were subject to savage air bombardment. One raid killed 11 of Basayev's own relatives. Meanwhile the West remained entirely indifferent to the Chechens' plight.[35] On the eve of a meeting of the G7, Basayev launched a spectacular expedition into southern Russia culminating in a mass hostage crisis at the town of Budyennovsk. Basayev and his fighters escaped into Chechnya. This was a massive blow to Moscow in the midst of what was already a deeply unpopular war. But it was an act born of isolation, despair and weakness. Basayev's own explanation for his action is significant:

> Before, I was not a supporter of that sort of action...because I knew what measures and cost it would entail... But when last year we were thrown out of Vedeno, and they had driven us into a corner with the very savage and cruel annihilation of villages, women, children, old people, of a whole people, then...[we said] 'Let's go to Russia...we will stop the war or we will all die'.[36]

The siege at Budyennovsk was followed by another in Daghestan, led by Dudayev's nephew, Salman Raduyev. This lost the Chechens popular sympathy in Daghestan and reinforced the propaganda images from Moscow. Nonetheless, opposition to the war in Russia and within the army was intense and Moscow was forced to conclude a truce in the run up to the elections. By the summer of 1996 resistance had revived. The course of war turned and finally Russia was forced to sign a peace deal. The issue of formal independence was deferred and Aslan Maskhadov became leader following the successful assassination of Dudayev by the Russians.

But the tensions over future strategy remained. Basayev and Maskhadov were divided over whether to try and reach some form of *modus vivendi* with Russia or take a more militant and hostile stance. The 1997 presidential elections were essentially fought along these lines with Maskhadov standing as the moderate against Basayev. Maskhadov won 60 percent, reflecting the overwhelming desire for peace and reconstruction, but Basayev still won 26 percent of the popular vote. In fact, their differences did not lead to an immediate breach and Basayev was appointed as Maskhadov's deputy. But their strategy was premised on the restoration of subsidies and (legal) trade with Moscow, and above all upon the reopening of the oil pipeline as the channel for the new reserves from the Caspian. The subsidies did not materialise. Those that did simply lined the pockets of the Chechen and Russian elite. Hopes for the pipeline were dashed as the alternative Western-backed routes emerged bypassing Chechnya and Russia.

At a more fundamental level, the crisis faced by the Chechen leadership reflects a wider crisis in the politics and class character of national liberation struggles in the context of post-Cold-War imperialism. There is a constant tension between the opposition of Chechen workers to the Russian occupation and distrust of their own bourgeois leadership:

> For five months they haven't paid me for coming to work for their government— the only reason I come is to eat in the canteen. When we ask them for pay they reply, 'How can you think of money at a time when the nation is in danger?' And then I have to watch them stuffing themselves with food at their feasts, building palaces for themselves at our expense, and this has been going on for three years. God punish them![37]

Chechnya was now a state whose entire modern infrastructure had been destroyed. All hopes of reconstruction evaporated and all the old corrupt practices returned with interest. Beslan Gantemirov, mayor of Grozny, was jailed for appropriating 54 billion Russian roubles intended for reconstruction and was rumoured to have had a personal oil quota of 100,000 tonnes. (He has now been released by acting president Vladimir Putin to form a pro-Russian militia.) In parts of the country sheer gangsterism took hold and desperate youth who had known only war and unemployment resorted to crime and abductions.

Basayev broke with Maskhadov and began to rebuild his guerrilla forces. Increasingly, more Chechens began to articulate their struggle in the language of Islam, particularly the young. Islam had not been strong in Chechnya prior to the war and zealotry had always been looked upon askance by most of the population. Even during the war most Chechens remained extremely cynical about the trappings of religious piety adopted by their leaders, the ever growing length of their beards, and their evident self enrichment.[38]

> We listen to the radio and watch TV. Now we realise that our leaders and the Russian leaders are really singing from the same hymn sheet. They wrap themselves up in Islam but it's just a cover for them to make money. [39]

But in the absence of any other world view Islam did begin to take greater root. It seemed to give expression to Chechen aspirations for freedom and independence whilst articulating a wider pole of unity beyond Chechnya's borders.

Basayev seems largely to have avoided being caught up in the institutionalised corruption of the Chechen elite by 'taking to the hills'. In what was perhaps not an unconscious imitation of Guevara's own endeavour to spread the liberation struggle, Basayev united with the mysterious Khattab in an attempt to spread resistance to Russia across the mountain republics of the north Caucasus. This moved the emphasis increasingly away from Chechen nationalism to pan-Islamism. In August 1999 Basayev and Khattab launched a joint expedition across into Daghestan with the hope of rousing the population against a corrupt local regime and spreading the revolt beyond Chechnya's borders. The attempt ended in disaster with ordinary Daghestanis arming themselves against the Islamic rebels. Moscow used the raid to full effect as a pretext to justify renewed invasion.[38]

It is not possible to be certain of the outcome of the current war. It is still too early to tell how far war weariness and disillusion with the post-independence regimes have fractured the cohesion of the Chechen population or undermined their determination to resist. Russia, however, has cause to fear for the long term fate of its most recent military adventure in Chechnya. Basayev and Maskhadov have again united their forces and it is clear that hatred of the Russian occupation remains unabated.

Conclusion

> Russia's territorial integrity is in greater danger now than before. Russia has, in effect, suffered humiliating military and political defeat. This can please only separatists and morally degraded people who hate the words 'patriotism' and 'statehood'... One thing is clear, it is not the end of the tragedy. The Russian state is still in danger. **Boris Fyodorov, former finance minister and free-marketeer at end of first Chechen war**

*The Russian army is reviving in Chechnya, faith in the army is growing and a politician who does not think so cannot be regarded as a Russian politician. In this case there is only one definition—a traitor. **Anatoly Chubais, former finance minister and free-marketeer at beginning of second Chechen war***

The final year of the 20th century closed with the two major powers of the Cold War launching brutal wars that claimed thousands of civilian victims in two regions that rank as the most unstable casualties of the Soviet collapse. The Balkans and the Caucasus face one another across the Black Sea, forming opposite ends of an arc of tension and instability that stretches from the southern underbelly of central Europe, through Turkey, to the southernmost borders of Russia. A new fault line has appeared along the very frontiers of the major powers and 'the Great Game' of the 19th century has returned to haunt us.

The response of the two camps to each other's militarism has been marked by cynicism and cant. Madeleine Albright, US secretary of state, recently described Russian acting president (and ex-KGB chief) Putin as 'a problem-solving patriot'.[40] NATO's cup of humanitarian concern quickly ran dry when it came to the Chechens. In fact, both NATO and Russian strategies have been remarkably similar, whether cloaked as 'humanitarian intervention', or combating 'rogue' and 'bandit' states or 'international terrorism'.[41] The connection runs deeper still. NATO's intervention in the Balkans and its expansion eastwards undermined the popular opposition to militarism within Russia itself that was so critical in forcing an end to the first Chechen war. Finally, war and the crisis of the free market march hand in hand. The south east Asian crash that spread to Russia in the summer of 1998 plunged millions of ordinary Russians deeper into poverty and fuelled the despair upon which militarism and chauvinism have grown.

Yet Russia's rulers are playing a high risk game. Workers' contempt for their rulers has not dissipated. Mistrust runs deep. Depite support for the war running at 70 percent in the polls, most believe that the most reliable source of information on the war comes from the Chechens themselves! The conditions that gave rise to the mass opposition to militarism witnessed during the first Chechen war remain. Half the population are in dire poverty. The corruption, criminality and ostentatious display of wealth on the part of the elite are everywhere in evidence.

However, as the world's imperialist powers seek every opportunity to extend their reach at each other's expense and lesser regional powers vie for dominance, armed intervention risks unpredictable outcomes and ever growing instability. The US is attempting to scrap the 1972 Anti-Ballistic Missile Treaty and Russia has been rattling its nuclear arsenal.

Therefore much is at stake. The Chechens are confronting the new post-Cold-War imperialism at its most vile. Once known only as a small and distant land—if known at all—Chechnya is now, for the worst of reasons, a household name. But its people are still referred to in the idioms of 19th century travelogue and racist prejudice. We are presented with images of a mountain people, a warrior tradition or, less romantically, bandit clans, vendetta codes and mafia crime. To these has been added the inevitable ingredient of fundamentalist Islam, and of course, its brother in arms—terrorism.

The left must be unequivocal in its response. For two centuries the Chechens have fought the Russian Empire. They are in every sense an oppressed nation. They were forged, and have forged themselves, on the anvil of modern imperialism. Their struggle for self determination is not a throwback to the past, but an act of resistance against the new world order. As Marx supported the struggle of the 'Mountaineers' and the wider struggle against the Great Powers during the 19th century, and as the left supported the liberation struggles in Algeria and Vietnam, so we should support the Chechens today. Their victory would be a vital blow to imperialism and the new world order.

The Chechens, however, face tremendous odds. If they win their independence they will still face the overwhelming economic might of an imperialist world order, and the oppression of class rule. Yet here the Chechens have a powerful ally. The Chechens and the international working class, both in Russia and beyond, face a common foe. It is in mobilising that force that the deadlock can be broken, and the struggle for self determination united with the struggle for socialism.

Notes

I would like to thank Dave Crouch and John Rees for their comments and suggestions.

1   Lermontov and Tolstoy fought in the Tsar's armies. Lermontov was at the massacre of Valerik. In providing a more or less literal translation I'm afraid Lermontov's poetic structure has been lost.

2   As many as 2,000 troops died on New Year's Eve. See C Gall and T de Waal, *Chechnya: A Small Victorious War* (London, 1997), p16. For accounts of the fighting in Grozny see ibid, pp1-19 and pp204-228; also A Lieven, *Chechnya: Tombstone of Russian Power* (New Haven and London, 1999), pp108-117.

3   Ibid, pp314-315.

4   J F Baddeley, *The Russian Conquest of the Caucasus* (Richmond, 1999).

5   On the eve of emancipation from serfdom in 1861 only 2 percent of the population were serfs. The absence of a feudal class structure largely explains the prolonged resistance of the Chechens when compared to their neighbours, whose rulers were incorporated by the tsars. See F Kazemzadeh, 'Russian Penetration of the Caucasus', in T Hunczac, *Russian Imperialism* (New Jersey, 1974), p255.

6   J F Baddeley, op cit, p148.

7   F Kazemzadeh, op cit, p253.

8   J F Baddeley, op cit, p402.

9   Sufiism is a mystical, ascetic branch of Islam whose adherents assert their own union with God.

10   J F Baddeley, op cit p287.

11   Ibid, p261.

12   Ibid, p479.

13   A Lieven, op cit, p317.

14   M Broxup, 'The Last Ghazawat: The 1920-21 Uprising', in M Broxup (ed), *The North Caucasus Barrier* (New York, 1992); and E Mawdsley, *The Russian Civil War* (London, 1987), pp225-226. Samursky was later executed by Stalin.

15   It might seem bizarre that the Bolsheviks were so permissive towards *sharia*. In fact it reflected a recognition that obscurantism could only be challenged by a break with great Russian chauvinism. In the north Caucasus in particular *sharia* had taken root as a means of marshalling the struggle against tsarist oppression.

16   A Autorkhanov, 'The Chechens and Ingush During the Soviet Period and its Antecedents', in M Broxop, op cit, p165.

17   Ibid; and A Lieven, op cit, p318. This was part of a purge of national leaderships across the Soviet republics. See T Cliff, *State Capitalism in Russia* (London, 1996), pp259-264.

18   W Flemming, 'The Deportation of the Chechen and Ingush Peoples: A Critical Examination', in B Fowkes, *Russia and Chechenia: The Permanent Crisis* (Basingstoke and London, 1998), pp72-74 and 82; and C Gall and T de Waal, op cit, pp59-61. The victims included relatives of Dhokar Dudayev, the first president of independent Chechnya.

19   The Ingush, however, were never granted their territory back in full and the dispute led to savage ethnic cleansing of the Ingush from North Ossetia in 1992.

20   This understates the proletarianisation of the Chechens, since housing in Grozny was disproportionately awarded to Russians. Many Chechen oil workers, for example, had to be bussed in from surrounding villages.

21   At the end of the 19th century the Caucasus provided 30 percent of the world's oil trade. During the Nazi-Soviet pact Soviet oil accounted for a third of Germany's imports.

22   For a sharp analysis of the significance of GUUAM and NATO expansion, see J Rees, 'NATO and the New Imperialism', *Socialist Review*, June 1999, pp17-19. The competitive dynamic of commercial and strategic interests leads to a complex rivalry between the minor and major players in the region. However, the underlying dynamic, irrespective of the immediate intentions of those involved, is towards instability and conflict. The most incisive, albeit partisan, analysis of the re-emergent 'Great Game' is to be found in R Forsythe, *The Politics of Oil in the Caucasus and Central Asia* (Oxford, 1996). Forsythe was Director of Russian, Ukranian and Eurasian Affairs at the US National Security Agency, 1993-1995.

23   See T Cliff, op cit, p264. The original 1947 manuscript was entitled *The Nature of Stalinist Russia*.

24   For an analysis of the collapse of the USSR and the national question see C Harman and A Zebrowski, 'Glasnost—Before the Storm', *International Socialism* 39 (Summer 1988), pp30-34; and C Harman, 'The Storm Breaks', *International Socialism* 46 (Winter 1989), pp10-15.

25   C Gall and T de Waal, op cit, pp93-96.

26   Ibid, pp83-89; and A Lieven, op cit, p66.

27   Yeltsin won 80 percent of the vote in Chechnya and 99.7 percent in Ingushetia!

28   Crime and corruption in Chechnya were closely linked to the criminal activity of the Russian elite. As the economy collapsed, Chechnya became a conduit for trade

from the Middle East and a transit post for avoiding tax duty. Indeed the Russian government has itself relied upon the most criminal elements in Chechnya.

29 F Cuny, 'Killing Chechnya', *New York Review of Books*, 6 April 1995, cited in C Gall and T de Waal, op cit, p219.

30 A Lieven, op cit, p40.

31 These camps are again being used as torture and execution centres. See Patrick Cockburn's articles in *The Independent,* especially 'Chechens "Raped And Beaten" In Detention Camps', 10 February 2000, and 'New Evidence Of Torture And Abuse By Russian Soldiers', 17 February 2000.

32 A Lieven, op cit, p118.

33 Ibid, pp324-325.

34 'Hazing' and 'fragging' are endemic amongst the Russian forces. Two thousand Russian soldiers die each year at the hands of their officers and fellow soldiers or through suicide.

35 When Clinton was asked why he did not call on Russia to halt the war he replied, 'I would remind you that we once had a civil war in our country...over the proposition that Abraham Lincoln gave his life for, that no state had a right to withdrawal from our Union.' C Gall and T de Waal, op cit, p316.

36 Ibid, pp259-260.

37 A Lieven, op cit, pp82-83.

38 Basayev too mocked the fake Islamism of his opponents during the presidential elections and made great efforts to present a secular image. For a fascinating, informed and perceptive account of the Chechen struggle see G Derluguian, 'Che Guevaras in Turbans', *New Left Review* 237 (1999), pp3-27.

39 'Inside Chechnya', *Correspondent*, BBC News 24.

40 The bombings of apartment blocks in Moscow were used to galvanise support for the war. However, it is in my view unlikely that these had anything to do with the Chechens. There is no space here to enter into the detail, but I am now almost entirely convinced that the bombings were perpetrated by elements within the state apparatus.

41 *The Guardian*, 2 February, 2000.

42 NATO commanders and Russia's generals also seem to match each other's contempt for those who suffer the consequences of their warmongering. Echoing Russia's public insistence that the inhabitants of Grozny are perfectly safe, K-FOR Commander Klaus Reinhardt recently maintained that Serbs in Kosovo have themselves never been safer, and would be pouring back to their homes if it was not for the black propaganda of the UNHCR! (Interview, BBC World Service, 24 December 1999)

The Balkans' imperial problem

A review of Misha Glenny, **The Balkans 1804-1990** *(Granta, 1999), £25*

LINDSEY GERMAN

It is tempting to view the history of the Balkans as one long nightmare from which its inhabitants struggle unsuccessfully to awake. Misha Glenny's new book helps us to avoid that temptation, even though his history of the region over the past 200 years contains descriptions of many nightmarish incidents. But he succeeds in putting this history into a context, which begins to make sense of many of the events. The dominant theme of his book is that it is impossible to understand politics and history in the Balkans without understanding the role of the various empires controlled by the Great Powers and how they have used the region for their economic and political gain without any regard for the outcome of their policies. Glenny writes:

> *Before 1999, the Great Powers had intervened three times in the Balkans. The first was at the Congress of Berlin in 1878 when European diplomats agreed to replace Ottoman power by building a system of competing alliances on the Balkan peninsula. The second began with the Austro-Hungarian ultimatum to Serbia in the summer of 1914 and culminated in 1923 with the Treaty of Lausanne and the Great Population Exchange between Greece and Turkey. The third started with Italy's unprovoked attack on Greece in March 1940 and ended with the consolidation of unrepresentative pro-Soviet regimes in Bulgaria, Romania and a pro-Western administration in Greece.*

These three interventions were so destructive that they guaranteed the Balkans' relative economic backwardness, compared to the rest of Europe. And the relative violence that these interventions encouraged, often inflicted by one Balkan people on another, ensured the continuation of profound civil and nationalist strife. In the West, however, these events are rarely regarded as the result of external intervention. On the contrary, the Balkan countries are seen as culprits who force the reluctant outside powers into their unfathomable conflicts.[1]

The impact of capitalism

The Balkans came late and slowly to capitalist development, but could not escape the consequences of that development. The region covered by the Balkans did not develop at all in the way that western capitalism did. The history of northern Italy, the Low Countries, England, parts of Germany and France was one of the early development of merchant trade and with it the towns, universities, Protestant religions, plus the transformation of agriculture. Whether or not they were successful in becoming fully fledged capitalist powers, they did see fundamental changes in social relations, particularly the end of feudal dominance and the abolition of serfdom. In eastern Europe the pattern was very different with serfdom remaining dominant until relatively recently (in Russia it was only abolished in 1861). The capitalist class emerged in the west through the development of trade and the rise of the towns; its counterpart was far weaker in size and influence in the east. Many of these societies were therefore characterised by economic backwardness and alongside it a social and cultural backwardness which further hindered the growth of forces for change and progress.

But capitalism as it developed fully became increasingly a world system—nowhere could remain totally untouched by its economic system, the ideas which developed from it and the changes in social relations which capitalist production brought about. However, capitalist development was also combined and uneven development—it brought great changes and technological advance but had a very different impact on those societies in which it arrived later than it had on, say, England or Belgium. Glenny's book covers precisely the period when capitalism began to have its impact on the various countries and peoples of the Balkans. There were people in the region who were influenced and enthused by the ideas which developed with capitalism, in particular with the 18th century Enlightenment which became embodied in the demands of the French Revolution for liberty, equality and fraternity. The right of nations to freedom and independence was an idea that took root at the same time. Despite the weakness of nationalist ideas in the Balkans at the beginning of the 19th century, Glenny makes the point that both the Serbs and the Greeks did fight very early on for independence from the Ottoman Empire with the Serb Uprising from 1804 and the Greek War of Independence of 1821-1830. In this they were well in advance of their counterparts in more developed parts of western Europe. But the societies in which they found themselves were not strong enough to maintain themselves without some outside intervention:

The First Serbian Uprising began over half a century before the unification of Italy; the first modern Greek state was proclaimed 40 years before the unification of Germany. But the national identities of Serbs and Greeks were ill defined. Both national movements owed their success more to Ottoman decay than to their own inherent strength. To compensate for their political and economic weakness, the national elites sought support for their aspirations from the European powers. Herein lies the start of the Balkan tragedy—these were peasant societies poorly equipped to assimilate the ideas of the Enlightenment, and located at the intersection of competing absolutist empires. The result was a stunted constitutional development whose shortcomings would inevitably be exploited by the Great Powers as competition between them intensified in the region in the second half of the 19th century.[2]

The intensification of competition to which Glenny refers was a result of the varied and changing fortunes the different empires of Europe faced. The rapid pace of capitalist development itself impacted on these empires in different ways. German unification led to a massive increase in the economic power of the German Empire and a much greater push for influence in the Balkans at the expense of two old and decaying empires which had traditionally dominated and controlled the region— the Ottoman and the Austro-Hungarian. Italian unification had also shaved bits off the Austro-Hungarian Empire and led to Austria's renewed interest in Bosnia. Russia, itself a huge if declining empire with further interests in the region, aimed to unite Russian Orthodox Slavs in a pan-Slavist movement. Russia's war with the Ottomans in 1877 led to the creation of a massive Russian-influenced Bulgarian state, which brought Europe to the brink of war. It was only the Congress of Berlin in 1878, called by the 'honest broker' Bismarck as a means of redrawing the Balkans map in Germany's favour, which averted this. Instead it established a series of compromises which cut the size of 'big Bulgaria', and balanced Russia's influence by extending Austria's influence to Bosnia and the Sanjak.

It was clear from the Congress of Berlin that the future of the region would be dominated by the European Great Powers—both those immediately in the region and those like Britain and France which saw their strategic interests threatened by the other empires, especially by the rise of Germany. And after the congress competition rather than co-operation dominated Great Power interests in the region. This was partly for military and strategic reasons, since the Balkans were the area where the Great Powers collided geographically. But this was also the heyday of European imperialism as the capitalist powers fought one another to control and carve up the world's markets. Most famously this took place in the 'Scramble for Africa', where a whole continent was divided up by a handful of European powers; but the Balkans were also a region of increasing economic interest for the different empires. For example, the Treaty of Berlin that resulted from the congress obliged Serbia, Romania and Bulgaria 'to fund various rail-building projects and tender the contracts to specified foreign consortia'.[3] In Bulgaria this took the form of a quarrel between Britain, Russia and Austria about which railway line should be built and when.

The road to war

This period of intensified nationalism and competition in the area only exacerbated local differences and conflicts as the empires tried to build their economic and military influence, and the larger states in the region—Bulgaria, Greece, Serbia and Romania—developed strong armies and an enhanced nationalist identity. Glenny demonstrates how the empires continued their traditional strategy of using different groups against one another in order to shore up their rule. And they all accepted, whatever their other differences, that they had the right to intervene in the Balkans to ensure what they saw as 'stability'. The 20th century saw this intervention increase dramatically when rivalry between Austria and Russia over the control of Kosovo and Macedonia increased following Russia's humiliating defeat at the hands of Japan in 1904. At the same time Germany's alliance with the Ottoman Empire, constructed in order to further the former's interests in the Middle East, terrified Russia and Britain into alliance in order to weaken Turkey and so damage German expansion.

This was the background to the Balkan Wars which broke out in 1912-1913 and which were a bloody prefiguration of the world conflict which erupted in 1914. That the Balkans developed into an armed, strongly nationalist, military camp in the years leading up to the First World War was very much due to Western intervention. In 1906, for example, France lent the already indebted Serbian government still further money to buy arms, on condition that this arms spending took the form of an exclusive deal for Schneider-Creusot artillery:

*The Balkan armies were funded by Western loans, Western firms supplied
them with weapons and other technology, their officers were schooled and
organised by Frenchmen, Germans, Russians and Britons. The compulsion of
the new states to grab territory, with scant regard to the facts of demography
or history, reflected the practices of their Great Power neighbours, whose
arbitrary decisions at the Congress of Berlin had ensured that there was
plenty of territory to dispute.[4]*

The Balkan Wars, first between Montenegro, Serbia and Bulgaria
against the Ottomans, then between Serbia, allied with Romania, and
Bulgaria, were horrific. But, as Glenny points out, 'the Balkan states
were not the powder keg [leading to a general European war]... They
were merely the powder trail that the Great Powers themselves had laid.
The powder keg was Europe'.[5] The Austrian annexation of Bosnia-
Hercegovina in 1908 had further exacerbated both the inter-imperial
rivalries and the nationalist tensions in the region between Serbs, Croats
and Muslims.

The events of the years up to 1914 were increasingly tense internationally as the imperialist rivalries grew and various flashpoints around
the world pointed to a heightened probability of war. One measure of this
instability was that between 1900 and 1913, Glenny tells us, 40 heads of
state, politicians and diplomats were assassinated for political reasons:
'The Balkans recorded eight successful assassinations, including two
kings, one queen, two prime ministers and the commander in chief of the
Turkish army'.[6] The European powder keg exploded in 1914 in a war
which began with the assassination of an Austrian archduke in Sarajevo
but spread far beyond the immediate dispute to pull in all the European
empires. The war finished the Russian, Austrian, Ottoman and German
empires and changed forever the victorious powers of Britain and
France. The Balkans were very badly affected by the fighting, but
perhaps even more so by the way in which 'ethnic cleansing', as it is
called today, and straightforward murder of people because of a particular nationality became commonplace. The war ended in revolution.
Russia's empire collapsed in early 1917, and although the war dragged
on for another 18 months, Germany and Austria-Hungary then exploded
in revolution.

Revolution defeated

The aim of the Great Powers which had caused the war and spent the
lives of millions in prosecuting it was to avert this revolutionary wave at
all costs. The revolutions in Germany and Hungary were eventually
defeated. In the Balkans themselves there was widespread instability. In
Bulgaria there was repeated unrest, from food riots in 1917 to peasant

rebellion in 1918, and it continued until the revolutionary wave was finally defeated in Germany in 1923. A mass Communist Party was created in Bulgaria under the impact of the Russian Revolution and the revolutionary wave throughout Europe. Perhaps the major weakness of Glenny's book is that he pays too little attention to the Russian Revolution and its impact on ideas and political organisation throughout Europe. There was real excitement about what it meant in the Balkans, and the notion of international working class struggle was a strong counterpoint to ideas of nationalism and chauvinism. For example, the Croats were in favour of the Kingdom of the Southern Slavs in 1918.

Glenny tends to concentrate on politics from above, rather than the left and movements from below. He does describe these politics very well, however. He shows how the Treaty of Versailles and its associated treaties were the crucial attempt by the victorious powers to redraw the boundaries of Europe, in the process advancing their own interests and rewarding their allies. The Balkans suffered particularly from the effects of Versailles for, despite the high flown claims of US president Woodrow Wilson that national interests would be safeguarded, there was little principle or consistency in the carve up. Brazil, Glenny points out, had three delegates to the peace conference despite having contributed only two torpedo boats to the war, while both Serbia and Belgium, which had been all but wiped out, had only two. Russia was excluded altogether since the victorious powers were engaged in a war of intervention against its revolutionary government. The main aim of the conference was to make Germany pay in territory and reparations for the war. The aims of achieving democracy throughout Europe as a result of the treaty sounded fine as abstract declarations, but the sort of democracy Wilson wanted had little to do with the rights of small nations to self determination. Rather its aim was to make the continent safe for further capitalist development and so was in direct contradiction to the attempts at working class and peasant revolution that had taken place in the defeated empires.

Italy, the new regional power which attempted to fill the breach left by the old empires, tried to influence the borders of the new state of Yugoslavia, as well as Albania and Turkey. It was allowed to throw its weight about by trying to prevent recognition of Yugoslavia, occupying some of the territories of the new country and annexing Fiume, an act supported by the fascist soon to be dictator Mussolini. The loss of much Yugoslav territory from the new state to Italy only exacerbated tensions between Serbs and Croats, who felt that Croatian land had been abandoned. The country's new constitution was regarded as a centralising one for Serbs and, therefore, the seeds of further tensions were sown.

Most horrendous of the effects of Versailles on the Balkans, however, was what Glenny calls the great catastrophe between Greece and Turkey.

Here too Italy had expansionist aims—to pick off parts of the Ottoman Empire. In order to prevent this, Britain proposed that Greece should occupy the city of Smyrna (Izmir), a port in Anatolya which gave access to the Middle East reserves of oil. This was obviously likely to lead to war with Turkey—a war which Greece was unlikely to win and which would cause immense harm to the Greek population there, who tended to live on the Anatolian seaboard. In fact, as Glenny recounts, when the tragedy ended three years later:

> ...the Pontic Greeks, with their indescribable wealth of cultural tradition stretching back to Homeric times, had been ripped almost literally overnight from their homelands; old Greece had been reduced to economic rubble and suffered political and social dislocations whose effects would be felt for decades; thousands upon thousands of Turkish, Greek and Armenian civilians were dead, and had been subjected to barbarous cruelty. Yet the tragedy was prolonged still further by the diplomatic negotiations at Lausanne which finally brought an end to the Great War for Greece and Turkey as late as 1923. Here, all parties, with the solemn blessing of Lord Curzon whose wish to become Foreign Secretary had finally been granted, agreed to the compulsory exchange of almost two million Greek and Turkish people.[7]

The war was brutal enough but its aftermath was more dreadful than anything seen in the Balkan wars of the late 20th century. Greece was eventually defeated, abandoned by its erstwhile big power allies and unable to sustain a war in Turkey; as it retreated the fate of the Greek and Armenian nationals in Smyrna was terror and death. By 3 September 1922 an estimated 30,000 refugees were arriving in the city every day, fleeing the Turkish army. It was at this point that the Great Powers decided to maintain their neutrality and not interfere with the Turkish conquest, even though there were British, French, US and Italian ships in Smyrna's harbour. On 9 September the Greek archbishop was murdered by a Turkish mob egged on by the Turkish military commander. Then Turkish troops sealed off the Armenian quarter, destroyed every house, raped many women and killed large numbers. Many Armenians who tried to escape at the harbour jumped into the sea and drowned or were shot by Turkish troops.

The Great Population Exchange agreed the following year at Lausanne meant that 1.3 million would be expelled from Turkey to Greece, while 800,000 Muslims would go from Greece to Turkey. 'Under the eye of Britain's senior diplomat, two Balkan nations agreed to end a conflict that British diplomacy had inspired, by setting a terrible precedent. It would be decades before the Greeks would properly recover from the Great Population Exchange; but the principle of partition and forced removal would be imitated again and again.[8]

The ensuing peace negotiations did not usher in a period of stability. The next two decades until the outbreak of the second global war of the century were ones of intermittent wars, dictatorship and fascism, mass unemployment, despair and misery. The economic weakness of the Balkans and the legacy of the Great Power interventions ensured that the region received its share of these problems. Greece was decimated by its war and took many years to recover. The national question continued to plague many countries: in greater Romania, for example, nearly a third of the population were non-Romanians. Countries such as Yugoslavia were dominated by agriculture, but much of its resources went into defence spending. Across the whole of the Balkans (apart from Bulgaria which was allowed only a token defence force under the Treaty of Neuilly) between 34 and 50 percent of national budgets were spent on the military. Yugoslavia fell to dictatorship within a few years of being established as a supposedly democratic state. Albania was effectively controlled by Mussolini's Italy, bolstering the rule of the corrupt King Zog. And 'the impact of the Wall Street Crash on the Balkans via Germany proved a challenge too far for democracy. In quick succession, the landowners, civil servants and generals throughout the Balkans backed dictators, royal and republican, to ensure stability against the rising danger of peasant radicalism'.[9]

Fascism and war

The two fascist dictatorships in Europe intervened in the Balkans— Mussolini sought to enforce Italian interests and territorial expansion, while Hitler's Germany was the only major European power prepared to invest as a means of ensuring its economic expansion. By 1936 the area was strongly dependent on the German economy. Fascism's influence extended in oil rich Romania through the anti-Semitic Iron Guard. The image of the Balkan countries portrayed in the novels of Graham Greene or Eric Ambler—of spying, intrigue, repression and palace coups—dates from this period. And the right wing repressive dictatorships that increasingly dominated the economically poor and backward region allowed some of the worst horrors of the Second World War to occur in the area. The Axis and the Allied powers both ensured that the Balkans became a cockpit of war once again, with terrible consequences for the ordinary people of the region. In Yugoslavia invading Germans bombed Belgrade in April 1941, killing 17,000 in a matter of hours. They also decided to back the Croatian fascists of Ante Pavelic's Ustashe, which comprised no more than 360 people when it took power. Glenny argues that 'the installation of Pavelic's brutal fascist regime resulted in the single most disastrous episode in Yugoslav history, whose consequences were still being felt in the 1990s'.[10]

The brutality of Nazi occupation and home grown fascism in the Balkans is breathtaking even by the standards of the history of the Second World War, and Glenny tells the story very well. In Greece people starved because of food shortages. In Yugoslavia concentration camps were established. 'From the Wehrmacht's meticulously recorded deportation of Salonika's 50,000 Jews to the random hell created by the Ustashe in the Croatian camps, the Final Solution in the Balkans was improvised according to local conditions'.[11] The mass resistance movements that grew up in Greece and Yugoslavia were a reaction to the hell of Nazi occupation and were civil wars between left and right.

Events outside the Balkan countries determined their fate, however. The agreement between Churchill and Stalin in 1944 planned the partition of Europe between the Great Powers, with Stalin maintaining influence over the eastern states, the British and Americans in the west. Greece was to remain under Western influence at Churchill's insistence, while influence in Yugoslavia was to be shared between the two. In Greece, British military intervention ensured the defeat of the left. The left was ideologically disarmed, as it was in other 'Western sphere' countries such as Italy and France, by the politics of Stalinism which were totally opposed to any revolutionary overthrow of the system. In Eastern Europe, Stalinist regimes were established effectively by the Red Army. In Yugoslavia Tito's partisans were eventually victorious. They had remarkable success in uniting the various nationalities, as Gabriel Kolko described in *The Politics of War*:

Tito had won the mass backing of the larger part of all Yugoslavs, whether Serbs, Montenegrins, Macedonians, or Croats, because he appealed to a pan-Slav nationalism, federal principles, and equality which promised a unified nation and social progress for the first time. The attraction was irresistible, and by its very nature applicable to much of the south Balkans. There was a potential expansionism, perhaps even imperialism, in Titoism which the Russians instantly recognised as a challenge to whatever position—passive or dominant—they would define for themselves in the area... No later than April 1944 the Yugoslav Communists spoke of a Balkan federation that would include Bulgaria and Albania as a start, and they had vaguely talked of autonomy for Macedonia within a federal state, which would also include a portion of the population of northern Greece with the same ethnic background as well... The Russians, it now seems certain, by the end of 1944 were instructing the Bulgarian Communists not to agree to the Yugoslav plans for a south Slav federation in the Balkans. In brief, the pan-nationalist key to Tito's success threatened to absorb much more than the territory of Yugoslavia, and to challenge Russian pre-eminence in south east Europe.[12]

Yet again the attempts at organising across national and ethnic lines were subjugated to the needs of the Great Powers rather than to those of ordinary people. Similarly, at the conference to determine the post-war settlement between the Allies at Yalta in 1945, Stalin openly colluded with British repression of the Greek popular movement saying, according to the conference's minutes, that 'he had no intention of criticising British actions there or interfering in Greece', to which Churchill, no doubt gratefully, responded that he was 'very much obliged to Marshal Stalin for not having taken too great an interest in Greek affairs'.[13]

The post-war settlement did indeed achieve a period of stability in the region. The Tito regime, which soon broke with Stalin, established a fairly successful state capitalist economy and was able for a relatively long period to govern a Yugoslavia where national tensions seemed relegated to secondary questions. The establishment of the Iron Curtain through the middle of Europe meant that for some decades the Balkans were no longer at the point where empires clashed. The long economic boom of the post-war years also provided a period of economic stability. But, as Glenny demonstrates throughout his history, this was in many ways an exceptional period, rather than typical of Balkan history over the past two centuries. While the centralised command economies in Eastern Europe were able to grow in the 1950s and 1960s, they increasingly found themselves unable to compete with the internationalised global economies which developed in the West. The contradictions of the regimes also led to political protest, most notably in Poland in the early 1980s where the Solidarity movement's challenge to the country's rulers heralded the beginning of the end for all the East European regimes. Within a decade they had all fallen.

The search for an alternative

The collapse of the regimes was unlamented by those who had suffered state repression, authoritarian rule, and gradual erosion of living standards and conditions. But the promises of the free market were not delivered—hence the continuing crisis in a whole number of the countries, most obviously and with the most barbaric effects in the former Yugoslavia. The collapse of the state-directed economy in the late 1980s led to the growth of workers' protests on the one hand and the resort to national 'solutions' by the former Communist leaders, most notably Milosevic and Tudjman, on the other. The wars of the 1990s were the result both of the eventual success of the nationalist arguments plus successive interventions of the Great Powers: over recognition of Slovenia and Croatia in 1991; over the bombing of the Bosnian Serbs in 1995 which facilitated the ethnic cleansing of the Krajina and led to the Dayton agreement with, among others, Milosevic and the effective colonial rule of Bosnia ever since. The latest chapter in this story is of course the 1999 bombing of Kosovo and Serbia in the name of humanitarianism, which had only exacerbated the problems in the area.

Glenny's book is an invaluable guide to understanding the roots of this recent history and should be essential reading for anyone who wants to dig deeper into the history of the area. It gives an overview of the region and prevents the catastrophe of Yugoslavia being seen as simply irrational. However, there are a few areas where the book is less than satisfactory. One is its sheer scope, which means absorbing vast amounts of detail about particular areas of the Balkans whose history may not be familiar. Although its range is obviously also a strength of the book, this makes it quite dense reading at times. In addition, Glenny's assessment of the latest war is a little ambiguous for someone who has such a clear eye about previous imperialist interventions in the region.

The weakest area of Glenny's analysis, however, is his omission of much detail about any alternative to the interventions or to the nationalist solutions which have so dominated the former Yugoslavia in recent years, and which threaten a number of other countries from Macedonia to Romania. Here it is worth returning to the tradition which was destroyed by Stalinism but which attempted to build socialist organisation on the basis of a Balkans federation that cut across national and ethnic boundaries. In 1914, when all the main socialist parties around Europe were leading the working classes of their respective countries into war, the Serbian Social Democrats were among the few who stood out against the imperialist carnage. On 31 July 1914 the Social Democrat Lapcevic, speaking against the granting of war credits in the Serbian parliament, said, 'When the costs of the war are assessed, the Great Powers will of course treat the small nations of the Balkans and Asia as mere objects to be handed out as compensation.' He demanded that Serbia 'cease to be a tool of the Great Powers, and pursue instead the goal of a Balkan federation'.[14] At the founding congress of the Communist International in 1919 Christian Rakovsky talked of the possibilities of revolution in the Balkans and advocated a Balkans socialist federation. A message from the Serbian Social Democrats talked of the enthusiasm for building revolutionary organisation among the different socialists in Croatia, Slovenia and Bosnia-Hercegovina.[15]

This tradition has been hidden. But working people throughout the Balkans have fought back on many occasions even in the recent past. The interventions of the West since the collapse of Communism have done nothing to solve the problems of the region, nor has the resort to nationalism which has led the people of the former Yugoslavia to a decade of war and misery.

If in the future the populations of the Balkans are to be able to control their history, rather than become prisoners of it, they have to rediscover this socialist internationalist tradition. It alone can point a way out of the problems of the region and provide a positive alternative to the present rulers and to the imperialist powers. Glenny's book has little to say on this subject. It would be useful therefore to read it in conjunction with the various accounts of the Communist International debates, with books like *The Politics of War*, which looks at Great Power policy at the end of the Second World War, or with David Fromkin's *A Peace to End All Peace,* which details the collapse of the Ottoman Empire after the First World War.[16] But, like all good histories, it gives a mass of information and insights that can help those socialists who want to bring this alternative nearer.

Notes

1   M Glenny, *The Balkans 1804-1999: Nationalism, War and the Great Powers* (London, 1999), p661.
2   Ibid, p39.
3   Ibid, p172.
4   Ibid, p221.
5   Ibid, p243.
6   Ibid, p303.
7   Ibid, p381
8   Ibid, p392
9   Ibid, p427
10   Ibid, p476
11   Ibid, p496.
12   G Kolko, *The Politics of War* (New York, 1990), pp135-136.
13   Ibid, p359.
14   J Riddell, *Lenin's Struggle for a Revolutionary International* (New York, 1984), p126.
15   J Riddell, *Founding the Communist International* (New York 1987), pp94-95 and pp292-296.
16   G Kolko, op cit; D Fromkin, *A Peace to End All Peace* (London, 1991).

The Russian civil war: a Marxist analysis

MEGAN TRUDELL

Against all odds the Russian Revolution fought off counter-revolution and foreign intervention for three years in a bloody civil war. Eighty years after that war's conclusion it is still a battleground for revolutionary socialists. The conflict remains a favourite target for right wing attacks on the Russian Revolution, and is a major focus of left wing critics who imprint their ideological confusion in the aftermath of the collapse of Stalinism onto the revolutionary period. The policies associated with War Communism—ending workers' control of the factories, requisitioning grain from the peasants and the constriction of democracy—are seen as the seedbed of forced industrialisation, collectivisation, the show trials and the gulag. A collection of documents from the civil war is introduced with this argument: 'The events of 1918-1922...foreshadow all the horrors of the Stalin period'.[1]

In assessing the trajectory of the revolution, however, it is important to separate similarities of form from social and political content. Clearly Stalin's regime in the 1930s *did* draw on measures introduced under War Communism in its drive to industrialise the Russian economy in competition with the West. Lenin and Trotsky were driving in a different direction in the hope that certain developments—international revolution most crucially—could have made dispensing with those temporary measures a real possibility. That they did not was no more 'inevitable' than the rise of fascism in Germany was an 'inevitable' result of the First World War because war economies existed in both.

The tragedy of the civil war is precisely that the impact of the war and isolation on Russian society increasingly reduced the scope of political decisions and choices available. The Bolsheviks' politics and organisation, and the conviction of the mass of workers and peasants in Russian society in the project they were embarked on, enabled them to continue to fight for the survival of the revolution for an astonishingly long time. But ultimately they could not break out of the cage of material circumstances, and neither could they remain unchanged by life as it really was.

The civil war begins

Marx wrote that men make history 'under circumstances directly encountered, given and transmitted from the past'.[2] The establishment of workers' power in October 1917 took place within the inherited circumstances of profound crisis at every level of Russian society.

In 1913, before the outbreak of the First World War, the average income in Russia was about a fifth lower than that of Britain at the end of the 17th century. The war made things worse. The decline in production that had begun in 1915 accelerated due to a lack of raw materials and the dislocation of transport.[3] In August 1917 the Putilov factory in Petrograd received only 4 percent of the fuel it needed to maintain production and by October had to close most of its workshops.[4] Shortages of supplies among the troops were commonplace as early as April 1917 and escalated sharply, so that by September 'the fronts, especially the Northern Front, were down to 10-20 percent of normal supplies of food', and disease and demoralisation spread.

Forced requisitioning in the areas nearest to the fronts was a common occurrence. This is a point most historians leave out of their accounts, but it is an important one. It indicates that requisitioning during the civil war by the Bolsheviks originated in a practical, rather than an ideological, response to hunger. As Marc Ferro explains, 'The Russian economy was collapsing before the October Revolution took place... The new regime had to rebuild from the ruins'.[5]

The consolidation of the revolution across the country, and the rebuilding of the economy to a sufficient level to generate a rise in living standards for the majority and guarantee soviet democracy was a herculean task. To attempt it in the heat of war, with fragile forces, was next to impossible.

The war was not initiated by the Bolsheviks. The October Revolution had begun the process of depriving the old ruling class of economic power through land decrees entitling peasants to seize the land, the nationalisation of the banks and the beginnings of workers' control of the factories. The balance of class forces in Russian society had shifted decisively, but the class struggle had not ended—it had become sharper and more polarised. As Morgan Phillips Price, writing for *The Manchester Guardian,* described the situation, 'The democracy has the vast majority on its side but the small body of industrialists and bankers is, with foreign assistance, fighting a stubborn battle for its existence as a class'.[6] Thus the civil war was a class war in which both sides were fighting for their survival—something that vast numbers of workers and peasants, not just Bolshevik Party members, recognised.

Revolution is not a single event but a process. Deepening and extending the revolution became utterly meshed with fighting a war for survival against the remnants of the overthrown class and their supporters. As Christopher Read, author of *From Tsar to Soviets*, puts it, the civil war was a 'complex process in which military and revolutionary development went hand in hand'.[7]

Initally the old ruling class was stunned and weakened by the revolution. It could rely on few forces, mainly tsarist officers and cadets whose morale was battered. It did nonetheless attempt to challenge the fragile forces of the new workers' state. By the end of 1917 a Cossack revolt led by General Kaledin at Rostov-on-Don became a beacon for counter-revolutionaries and was backed up by the forces of the Volunteer (White) Army. Still forming under generals Alexseev, Kornilov and Denikin, the Volunteer Army had only 3,000-4,000 men, among them the most experienced officers. The Bolsheviks themselves could muster only 6,000-7,000 inexperienced troops with 12 machine guns. Yet, as on so many occasions in the civil war, politics proved decisive. The Cossack troops split because those who had fought in the First World War were reluctant to fight again, and the Red forces were able to take Rostov in February 1918. In despair Kaledin shot himself, and the White forces were forced to flee. In April they were dealt another blow when Kornilov was killed in a Red artillery attack on his headquarters. Denikin assumed command and led a retreat back to the Don region.

Ten days after Kornilov's death Lenin was able to tell the Moscow Soviet, 'It can be said with certainty that, in the main, the civil war has ended...there is no doubt that on the internal front reaction has been irretrievably smashed'.[8] Yet a year later the Volunteer Army had grown to 100,000 well armed and highly trained troops, and came close to destroying the revolution. The Russian counter-revolution was able to rise from the ashes as a direct result of the intervention into the civil war of the major imperialist powers. As Lenin wrote later, 'From the continuous triumphal march of October, November, December on our internal front, against our counter-revolution...we had to pass to an encounter with real international imperialism...an extraordinarily difficult and painful situation'.[9]

The 'democratic' counter-revolution

The intercession of foreign powers into Russia was initially cloaked in support for a 'democratic' alternative to both the Bolsheviks and the old regime. The revolutionary process had driven moderate socialists, the Mensheviks and the Right Socialist Revolutionaries (RSRs),[10] into opposition. They argued that the bourgeois stage of the revolution—the establishment of parliamentary democracy under capitalism—had to be consolidated before the working class could maintain power. They responded to the actuality of workers' power by calling for the reconvention of the Constituent Assembly.

The Constituent Assembly, which revolutionaries had called for before October, had, in the swift moving political climate, become a focus for opposition to the soviets. After its dissolution in January 1918 the RSR leaders fled to Samara, west of the Urals on the Volga, and attempted to rally enough forces to reconvene the assembly and overthrow the Bolsheviks. Their chance came in May with the rebellion of 30,000 Czechoslovak troops who allied themselves with the RSR leaders, swept the fragile soviets aside, and established a base for a new Russian government calling itself the Committee of Members of the Constituent Assembly (KOMUCH).

KOMUCH wanted a non-Bolshevik democracy but had a tiny popular base and therefore relied on the Allies for support, in practice casting its lot in with the counter-revolution. It stated, 'KOMUCH includes as one of its basic tasks the merciless struggle against Bolshevism by forming armed forces and arming the people themselves...to carry out these aims KOMUCH will form a central organ of All-Russian government whose duty will be to carry out all executive functions and attract to its side *all the classes and peoples of Russia* [my emphasis]'.[11]

KOMUCH swiftly made clear that 'all the classes' meant the propertied classes. During its four month rule in Samara 4,000 mainly Bolshevik political prisoners were taken; the local (democratically elected) soviets were barred from political life; Bolsheviks were barred from the government and industry and banks were returned to their previous owners.

The weaknesses in KOMUCH quickly became apparent when the Czechoslovak forces withdrew from fighting altogether in October 1918. KOMUCH formed the People's Army, but only 8,000-10,000 volunteered, forcing them to conscript. The inaccurately named People's Army had perhaps 30,000 undisciplined troops at its height—despite the fact that KOMUCH was ruling over an area with a population of 12 million. The army 'headquarters became a stronghold of rightist and monarchist officers, a Trojan horse of White counter-revolution inside the democratic citadel'.[12]

Another anti-Bolshevik government was established at Omsk in Siberia. More right wing than KOMUCH and mutually hostile to it, it commanded an army of 40,000 which came quickly under the influence of White officers. Under pressure from the Allies, KOMUCH and the Omsk government formed an All-Russian government in September 1918. It established a five member Directory based at Omsk, which was empowered to *appoint* an All-Russian Provisional Government without democratic check. In just a few months the high ideals of a democratic alternative to the Bolsheviks had led to an undemocratic, unrepresentative rump, increasingly dependent on the White forces and the Allies.

The 'democrats' saw to it that Allied troops were looked after: 'The Omsk War Industry Committee has taken upon itself the task of equipping all those Allied troops which have already arrived in Siberia'.[13] In August 1918 accommodation was provided for British forces landing at Archangel, and in October the British General Knox arrived in Omsk from Vladivostok where he had been training White Admiral Kolchak's troops. Kolchak was appointed as the minister of war and on 17 November, almost certainly with Knox's help, led a coup to depose the Directory.

Thus the members of the 'democratic counter-revolution' opened the door for the genuine article and paid with their lives. When a Bolshevik uprising was suppressed a month after Kolchak had taken power 400 were killed. Fifteen political prisoners, all RSRs and members of the Constituent Assembly who had been freed by the revolt, gave themselves up to Kolchak's men and were taken out and shot without trial. The slogan of the Socialist Revolutionaries and Mensheviks in the revolution's first months had been 'neither Lenin nor Denikin (or Kolchak)', but as the trajectory of the Samara and Omsk governments shows, in the class war that raged in Russia there was no middle ground to stand on. The alliance of socialists with the Allies and bourgeoisie aided the right, and gave the Allies and Germany an excuse to intervene in Russia.

Foreign intervention

The standard historians' view of intervention is that it was a useful piece of propaganda for the Bolsheviks, not a central factor in determining the course of the war. Christopher Read, for example, argues that the support of foreign governments for the Whites 'was more helpful to the Bolsheviks, who portrayed the Soviet leadership as leaders of a national liberation struggle against foreign imperialists, than to the Whites, who failed to secure any lasting military advantage from it'.[14] 'Foreign intervention was halfhearted and ineffective',[15] according to the editors of

Documents from the Soviet Archives, a view supported by Richard Pipes, who claims, 'There was never anything resembling "imperialist intervention" in the sense of a concerted, purposeful drive of the Western powers to crush the Communist regime'.[16]

The facts, however, utterly disprove these protestations. The men, munitions, supplies and money that flowed to the White side prolonged the civil war immeasurably. Without such aid the counter-revolution would have been decisively crushed by early in 1918. Foreign intervention led directly to the loss of millions of lives through fighting, disease and starvation, all exacerbated by economic sanctions, and contributed significantly to the failure of revolutionary governments in Finland, Hungary and the Baltic states.

One historian of the civil war, Evan Mawdsley, argues that the 'military operations of the Central Powers from February to May 1918 were the most important foreign intervention in the civil war. Hundreds of thousands of German, Austrian and Turkish troops were involved; 17 Russian provinces (as well as Poland) were occupied'.[17] In the Ukraine the Red Army had captured Kiev from the nationalist, RSR-dominated Rada (council) in February 1918, only to be driven out by the German army which established a puppet government led by the vicious General Skoropadsky: 'Once in full occupation of the Ukraine the Germans hastened to turn the wheel of social revolution backwards'.[18]

The regime's policy of returning land to its previous owners provoked mass peasant resistance, as did widespread requisitioning by German forces. On official figures the Central Powers took 113,421 tons of grain, eggs, butter and sugar from the Ukraine before November 1918—illustrating that all sides in the civil war requisitioned. As well as occupying the Ukraine, Germany also aided the White Finns, taking Helsinki in April, and unleashed a brutal White terror.[19] Over 70,000 were interned in concentration camps and between 10,000 and 20,000 were murdered: 'Membership of a workers' organisation meant arrest, and any office in one meant death by shooting'.[20] In comparison, the Soviet revolution in Finland had cost under 1,000 lives.[21] Germany also assisted in the formation of Baltic White units, most notably the Northern Army based in Pskov, which would come close to invading Petrograd in 1919. As late as the summer of 1919, counter-revolutionaries were recruited in Germany and sent to the Baltic provinces with full uniform and promises of 'all they can get from the Jewish population when they get to Russia'.[22]

Accepting German culpability is more palatable to Mawdsley than admitting the Allied role in Russian affairs: 'The "14 power" anti-Bolshevik Allied alliance that was featured in Soviet propaganda was a myth'.[23] This is a quite astonishing statement. Allied intervention at the

level of funds, intelligence, arms, training and bodies of armed men on
Russian soil was a feature of the civil war from the very beginning. As
early as November 1917 General Labvergne, the head of the French
Military Mission, and a senior US officer had given official encourage-
ment to General Dukhonin at the army headquarters outside Petrograd.
France recognised the independence of the Ukraine under the anti-
Bolshevik Rada in December 1917 and loaned the Rada 180 million
francs.

There was very little direct engagement with Red forces by foreign
troops, mainly due to the continuation of the First World War. The
context of world war also conditioned the attitude of the foreign powers
to intervention in Russia. They were united against the Bolsheviks but
divided amongst themselves. Not only did each power have its own economic and territorial interests, but the potential for internal unrest in
most of the countries involved meant national ruling classes were
divided.

Britain, the country that made the most serious contribution to the
Whites, wanted to protect the Middle East from Russia and feared a
united Russia and Germany, especially after the German Revolution in
November 1918. Churchill and Lord Curzon were the most vitriolically
anti-Bolshevik politicians and wanted a major intervention against the
Soviet government, while others, including Lloyd George, vacillated, not
least as the temperature of the class struggle rose in Britain in 1919. The
latter was a decisive factor—together with unrest in Ireland, India and
Egypt—in British withdrawal from Russia in 1919.

British aid included providing the Whites with arms and material,
training White officers, providing spies and communications aid, and
sending naval contingents to the Baltic and the Gulf of Finland to
'defend' Estonia and Latvia and enforce the blockade against the
Bolsheviks. In July 1918 the British landed in Archangel in the north and
used their strategic positions in the seas to support the anti-Bolshevik
forces. The British 'decision to intervene, and to exploit the Black Sea
route, was taken before Kolchak's coup; but having taken a decision in
the name of democracy and humanity, the government seemed at first
happy enough to allow its forces to be used by the proponents of dictatorship and reaction'.[24] At the end of 1918 the British recognised the
independence of Azerbaijan and Georgia, both hostile to the Bolsheviks,
and sent troops to Baku to protect oil supplies and to prevent oil reaching
the Reds.

Intervention by France was guided by a desire to recoup lost invest-
ments in Russia as well as to create buffer states against attacks from
Germany. In March 1919 the 65,000-70,000 French troops were heavily
defeated by the Red Army and Ukrainian guerrillas at Kherson and at

Odessa. French soldiers at Sevastopol on the Crimea mutinied. 'Not one French soldier who saved his head at Verdun and the fields of the Marne will consent to losing it on the fields of Russia,' said one of their officers.[25] France evacuated its troops from Odessa in April, but intervention did not stop there: Polish leader Pilsudski's attack on the Ukraine in the spring of 1920 was aided by the French government, who gave him credits and munitions in return for the hoped-for goal of an enlarged Poland to threaten Germany from the east.

The US sent 7,000 troops to Siberia under the pretext of rebuilding the anti-German front, but also in response to the intervention of 70,000 Japanese troops. The Japanese were helped by Semenov and Kalmykov, two Cossack warlords, who 'under the protection of Japanese troops were roaming the country like wild animals, killing and robbing the people... If questions were asked about these brutal murders, the answer was that the people murdered were Bolsheviks'.[26]

Intervention was no myth: 'By the close of 1918 the interventionist forces in Russia had reached a total of nearly 300,000 men—French, British, Americans, Italians, Japanese, German Balts, Poles, Greeks, Finns, Czechs, Slovaks, Estonians and Latvians—in Archangel, Murmansk, Finland, Estonia, Latvia and Poland, as well as on the Black Sea, on the Trans-Siberian Railway, and at Vladivostok'.[27] Even those who insist it was a myth are clear that foreign aid made a crucial difference to the fortunes of the Whites. Richard Pipes states, 'The Whites...had to rely on weapons captured from the enemy and on deliveries from abroad. Without the latter, the White armies...would not have been able to carry on'.[28] Read concurs: 'It was only towards the end of 1918 and in 1919, when significant foreign intervention, in the form of supplies and troops, began to arrive that the attrition of the White forces came to a halt and they were able to go on the offensive in a major way'.[29]

After the signing of the Brest-Litovsk treaty in spring 1918, Russia was blockaded—a move justified by the need to prevent supplies reaching Germany. According to conservative historians the continuation of the blockade after the Germans signed the armistice had 'only symbolic importance',[30] and had 'little effect' since Russia had little to trade.[31]

There *was* very little for Russia to export, but that was true before the revolution. Although in 1914 Russia's exports had outweighed imports, 'Russia's much reduced production...was absorbed in its entirety by the war effort, leaving nothing available for export. In these conditions, Russian foreign trade by 1916 had dwindled to limited proportions, and was largely made up of supplies sent to Russia by her allies'.[32] The blockade was preventing the influx of aid not to Russia as a whole, but to the Bolshevik side in the class war. The Whites had nothing to trade either, yet supplies poured in to Kolchak and Denikin. Reports from Siberia while it was still under the control of the Directory detail the foreign supplies, including 100,000 train wagons from the US. Trade between the Whites and foreign powers continued despite the blockade. Between October 1918 and October 1919 Britain sent Omsk 97,000 tons of supplies, including 600,000 rifles, 6,871 machine guns and over 200,000 uniforms.[33] According to Pipes, 'every round of rifle ammunition fired by [Kolchak's] troops was of British manufacture'.[34]

Total Allied aid to Kolchak in the first months of 1919 amounted to 1 million rifles, 15,000 machine guns, 800 million rounds of ammunition, and clothing and equipment for half a million men, 'roughly equivalent to the Soviet production of munitions for the whole of 1919'.[35] By August 1919 Britain had already spent £47.9 million helping the Whites—rising to £100 million by the end of the year, a figure equivalent to approximately £2.5 billion today. The French contribution was only slightly less, while the US allowed 'considerable sums' it had granted Kerensky's government to be diverted to the White cause by the ambassador of the Provisional Government.[36] The imperialist powers may have left the frontline fighting to the Russian Whites, but Czechoslovak, Japanese, British, French, American, Polish, Romanian and Italian troops guarded the Trans-Siberian Railway to ensure supplies from Vladivostok reached Kolchak. A Siberian song at the time of Kolchak's rule expressed the situation perfectly: 'Uniform, British; boot, French; bayonet, Japanese; ruler, Omsk'.[37]

In a country where the productive forces were already devastated, the blockade, far from being symbolic, was a mortal blow. The journalist John Reed wrote, 'The conscious Allied policy of blockading Russia against medicines killed untold thousands'.[38] The historian E H Carr argues that the blockade was also a central factor in necessitating the continuation of War Communism: 'Soviet Russia's complete economic isolation at this time was a powerful contributory factor to economic experiments which could scarcely have been attempted or persisted in except in a closed system'.[39]

Even once the blockade was lifted in January 1920, following the defeat of foreign intervention in Russia, the Allied countries refused to accept Soviet gold as payment. The 'gold blockade' meant vital imports were denied to Russia. Under the tsarist regime 58 percent of industrial plant and 45 of percent of agricultural machinery had been imported. The collapse of industrial production and the production of agricultural machinery—for example, plough production in 1920 was 13 percent of its 1913 figure—desperately needed to be addressed, and the blockade compounded the situation.

In 1921 drought added to the catastrophe and the ensuing famine affected an estimated 33 million people and killed 5 million, principally in the Volga provinces of Kazan, Ufa, Samara and Orenburg, parts of the Southern Ukraine and the Don basin. Production in these areas declined by 85 percent of its pre-revolution figure, which was itself pitiful. In July 1921 Lenin reported to the Third Congress of the Comintern that 'the sufferings of the peasants became unbearable'. The situation was so desperate that an official Soviet government journal article in September 1920 argued, 'It will be necessary to export what we need ourselves simply in order to buy in exchange what we need even more. For every locomotive, every plough, we shall be obliged literally to use pieces torn out of the body of our national economy'.[40]

The only foreign aid to reach Russia was from the unofficial American Relief Administration but was withdrawn in 1922 by the future president Herbert Hoover, who was 'outraged' at 'the inhumanity of a government policy of exporting food from starving people in order that through such exports it may secure machinery and raw materials for the economic improvement of the survivors'.[41] Pipes hides away in his notes US historian Arthur Schlesinger's criticism of Hoover for holding the 'fantastic belief' that the US 'federal government should not ...feed starving people'.[42] No other country's ruling class contributed to famine relief.

Christopher Read describes Allied policy in Russia in terms that are all too recognisable today: 'Russia was the first test bed for what has become standard Western (that is, initially British and French, later in the century, American) counter-revolutionary tactics based on direct armed intervention where feasible, ample funding of contras if not, and "low intensity" (providing one is not on the receiving end) economic warfare in any case'.[43]

Foreign intervention also played a devastating role in the containment of the revolution within Russia's borders. Kolchak's push to the Volga in the spring of 1919 put an end to Red Army support for the new Baltic Soviet states, and Denikin's push through the Red lines in the summer prevented the Red Army from moving west to link up with Soviet Hungary. Without support from the Red Army 'local security forces and foreign intervention crushed the Soviet elements in the Central European revolutions'.[44]

The Bolsheviks understood that the only chance for the Russian Revolution to succeed in its goal of building a socialist society was as one stage in an international revolution. This would protect the workers' state from foreign intervention and reconcile the peasantry to the rule of the working class, bringing with it the impact of greater productive forces and gains in machinery, techniques and raw materials that could bind them to a workers' state. Lenin was convinced that 'the absolute truth is that without a revolution in Germany we shall perish.'

The possibility for the spread of revolution was very real. The years 1918-1919 were marked by social upheavals across Europe. However, social democratic leaders stepped into the vacuum on each occasion. The subjective weight and strength of revolutionary organisations across Europe in relation to that of social democratic parties was a central factor in the failure of Europe's revolutions to break through, but had the new workers' state in Russia not been contained for three years by the impact of intervention it could have aided revolutionary movements elsewhere which lacked its experienced leadership. William Chamberlin suggests that 'had there been no intervention, had Allied aid to the Whites stopped after the end of the [First World] war, the Russian civil war would almost certainly have ended much more quickly in a decisive victory of the Soviets. There a triumphant revolutionary Russia would have faced a Europe that was fairly quivering with social unrest and upheaval'.[45]

The combined impact of intervention in all its forms had a far greater bearing on the continuation of the civil war and on the choices the Bolsheviks were forced to take economically, politically and militarily than most historians ascribe to it. Psychologically, backing from the Allies gave the Whites a respectability and national standing that was far removed from their actual support in the country and increased the sense of Red isolation and, as historians are agreed, the Whites were not capable of sustaining themselves without outside aid. The world's ruling classes flung themselves behind the assorted monarchists, rightists and officers who had been overthrown, and enabled them to launch a counter-revolutionary onslaught. This ultimately ensured that Soviet Russia was unable to receive aid, sealed from revolutionary upheaval elsewhere. The strangulation and isolation of the revolution was the aim, and the eventual outcome, of foreign intervention.

Some histories of the civil war not only underplay the extent of intervention from foreign ruling classes but also tend to treat intervention as entirely separate from the choices and decisions made by the Bolshevik leadership during the war. This contributes to the analysis that the Bolsheviks' decisions were made primarily as a result of ideological commitment to them, rather than as responses to desperate circumstances. So Richard Pipes can write, 'The civil war was not forced on the Communist leaders by the foreign and domestic "bourgeoisie"; it lay at the heart of their political programme'.[46] However useful a tactic for giving weight to an argument, such compartmentalisation of factors during the war does not help us to gain any real insight. The point, surely, is to understand the way in which ideological and material factors connected.

Hopefully the preceding section has illustrated the extent of foreign responsibility for the civil war and gone some way to answering Pipes. The impact of intervention on the subsequent measures undertaken by the Bolsheviks cannot, in my view, be underestimated. Without wishing to undertake a 'what if?' argument, it is clear that the presence of hostile forces on Russian soil had a decisive part to play in the economic and military policies of the Bolsheviks. To understand how, it is necessary to examine the details of the civil war more closely.

1918

By the summer of 1918 'the obstacles facing the Soviet government seemed insurmountable'.[47] In May, miners defending the fledgling Soviet government at Rostov were defeated as the German army marched in alongside Whites under Colonel Drovodsky and the Don Cossacks. The anti-Bolshevik governments at Omsk and Samara were established, and British troops landed at Archangel, overthrew the soviet and set up a north Russian government. Baku in Azerbaijan was also occupied by the British. In the same month Denikin captured the Kuban territory in the south and the Japanese army landed in Vladivostok. The Bolshevik government, now based in Moscow for safety, was encircled by enemies. Trotsky later wrote that 'it seemed as if everything were slipping and crumbling, as if there were nothing to hold to, nothing to lean upon. One wondered if a country so despairing, so economically exhausted, so devastated, had enough sap left in it to support a new regime and preserve its independence'.[48]

In the face of sweeping German advances in early 1918 the pressure on the Soviet government heightened, and the fragile coalition government established with the Left Socialist Revolutionaries (LSRs) began to fracture. Desperate to create a breathing space in which to build up an army and consolidate the revolution, Lenin argued for peace with the Central Powers to end Russia's involvement in the imperialist war: 'We are now powerless. German imperialism has gripped us by the throat, and in the West I see no proletarian fists that will deliver us from the claws of German imperialism. Give me an army of a 100,000 men—but it must be a strong, steadfast army that will not tremble at the sight of the foe—and I will not sign the peace treaty'.[49] Ending the war had been a key platform for the Bolsheviks' support and the army was disintegrating, but signing the treaty isolated the Bolsheviks in government. The LSRs refused to countenance the treaty and, calling instead for a revolutionary war against Germany, left the coalition and embarked on terrorist activity to undermine Bolshevik rule. An uprising in Moscow and a military revolt led by Left SR officer Muraviev were put down, but were serious blows to the Bolsheviks who still had only a skeletal army.

Simbirsk and Kazan were captured by KOMUCH forces by August and half the store of the country's gold reserves were seized.

The Brest-Litovsk treaty stopped the German advance, but German occupation of the Ukraine and swathes of western Russia, as well as Poland, Lithuania and Latvia, deprived Soviet Russia of nearly a third of its population, 80 percent of its iron production, 90 percent of coal production and about 50 percent of all industrial plant and equipment. The German army occupied one of the country's most grain-rich areas, cutting off supplies. In addition, the railway system was in tatters; in January 1918, 48 percent of rolling stock was out of action, seriously affecting the transportation of what food there was from Siberia and the Volga. William Chamberlin writes that the 'fight for bread was the fight for the very existence of the Soviet regime'.[50]

The lack of fuel and raw materials produced factory closures and mass unemployment, as high as 80 percent in Petrograd. Rocketing inflation and rationing led to the growth of the black market. Malnutrition and disease were widespread: 'The most dreaded epidemic scourges, typhus and cholera, stalked hand in hand with cold and hunger through the dreary and forlorn cities of Soviet Russia'.[51] Many workers fled to the countryside in search of food—between 1914 and 1920 the population of Petrograd fell by 66 percent, that of Moscow by 42 percent and of Kiev by 30 percent.[52] Lenin wrote at the time, 'Unavoidable catastrophe is threatening Russia... The railways will come to a standstill...unemployment has assumed a mass scale... We are nearing ruin with increasing speed. The war will not wait and is causing increasing dislocation in every sphere of national life'.[53]

These circumstances forced the Bolsheviks to take decisions far removed from the socialist ideal. The nationalisation of industry and the introduction of one man management replaced the factory committees' autonomy—a backward but crucial step as competition between factories made a coordinated response to the needs of the army impossible. In addition, capitalists and managers resisted the threats to their property and put up widespread resistance to the new government: 'The failure of such relations to evolve led to the withdrawal of managers and owners and exacerbated the collapse of factories, industries and whole economic sectors that, in turn, necessitated complete worker takeover and increasing state involvement as a last resort'.[54] The dislocation of industry had a direct bearing on agrarian policy. The requisitioning of surplus grain from the peasants to feed the troops and the working class was necessary given the collapse of trade and the twin barriers of occupation and blockade. It was also a policy every army on Russian soil was driven to, as frontlines were often miles from supply bases, and transport was severely damaged.

Mawdsley argues the belief that 'the economic mistakes of early 1918 led to the civil war…is certainly more true than saying that this fighting led to the economic mistakes',[55] but in the context of the threat to the revolution the options were severely limited, conditioned not only by the class priorities of the Bolsheviks but by the resistance of the old order. As Lenin argued in 1921, 'War and destruction forced "War Communism" upon us. This policy was not and never could be in accordance with the economic mission of the proletariat. It was merely a provisional measure'.[56] There is no doubt that the policies of War Communism did not promote coherent economic reconstruction in Russia, but as the revolution's choices were reduced to surviving the war at all costs or being beheaded by reaction those policies ensured the army could continue to fight—the absolute priority was met.

Yet if the Bolsheviks had faced widespread protest and revolt from the working class as a result of their policies they could not have continued. Repression alone could not have provided a social base from which to fight the civil war. The response of workers to severe hardship is instructive—there were protests, but where they occurred in towns workers were more likely to be rioting out of hunger than out of disagreement with Bolshevik ideas,[57] for two interconnected reasons: the vast majority did not want to see the Whites win and restore a system that was nearly universally despised, and the impact of the revolutionary experience had altered workers' political consciousness fundamentally. As Chamberlin writes, 'Revolution is not an automatic reaction to a given amount of suffering. The spirit and character of the government in power, and of the forces in opposition to it, may be of decisive importance'.[58] Ideas are not transformed simply in relation to economic and material factors—the aims and motives of the revolution continued to burn strongly under the conditions of fighting and sacrifice. The Bolsheviks maintained support throughout the civil war period because those millions who had fought on the streets for the revolution, whose consciousness now held the possibility of the construction of a socialist society, would defend that vision and continue to fight for it at least for as long as the choice between revolution and reaction was so starkly drawn.

The Red Army

The priorities of the Soviet state were bound up with those of its army for the duration of the civil war. The shape of the Red Army was dictated in large part by the contradiction in which the revolution was caught—the necessity of fighting against a modern, well-equipped enemy entailed the construction of a serious fighting force, yet socialist ideals had to be ingrained in the men and women who joined the army. The history of the army, its formation, growth and nature exemplify the continual battle to spread the revolution and fight for socialism in an embattled and crisis-ridden society.

Some historians have identified a continuity in the militarism of Soviet society that ran from the civil war through to the subsequent Stalinist regime. Mark von Hagen, for example, argues that the 'discourse of the show trials of the 1930s is one example of the fundamental reorientation of political culture that had been occurring at least since the mid-1920s, *and arguably since 1917*' [my emphasis].[59] It is true that the massive size and importance of the army distorted the ideals of the revolution and that many of the Red Army soldiers were to become key elements in the Stalinist bureaucracy. However, there is no seamless connection between the army built to defend the revolution and that which fought the Battle of Stalingrad in 1942 or invaded Hungary in 1956. Leon Trotsky, who, as Commissar for War, was put in charge of creating an armed force that could defend the revolution, argued that 'the army is a copy of society and suffers from all its diseases, usually at a higher temperature',[60] and even a brief examination of the army shows the extent to which it reflects the priorities of the state. The army alone did not dictate the trajectory of the Soviet state; rather, the fate of the army was interlaced with the strangulation of the Russian Revolution.

The First World War had left an estimated 7 million Russians dead, wounded or imprisoned out of 16 million mobilised—40 percent of the male population between the ages of 15 and 49. The Bolsheviks quickly realised that the old army could not be preserved and rebuilt in the interests of the new state, and encouraged soldiers to lay down their arms and go home. Even before the October Revolution the tsarist army had been disintegrating. After the revolution it melted away. As Trotsky described in his military writings, 'The revolution grew directly out of the war, and one of its most important slogans was for the ending of the war...yet the revolution itself gave rise to new dangers of war, which kept increasing'.[61] But the army did not want to fight: 'It had carried out a social revolution within itself, casting aside the commanders from the landlord and bourgeois classes and establishing organs of revolutionary self-government...[measures] necessary and correct from the standpoint of breaking up the old army. But a new army capable of fighting could certainly not grow out of them'.[62]

The earliest organised defence of the revolution was a volunteer army made up of the workers' militia, the Red Guards, which numbered around 40,000 in October 1917—3,000-4,000 of them under arms—and about 100,000 volunteers. The only significant force was the 35,000 strong Latvian Rifle Brigade. This was not a regular army; the Red Guards served in rotation and elected their commanders. In the surviving army units the soldiers' committees lived on. It is incredible, and testimony to the weight of revolutionary hopes among the soldiers, that they could be persuaded to fight at all after the murderous years on the Eastern Front. But these combined forces were inadequate in the face of the organised might of the Germans or Czechoslovaks. In February 1918 the Red Guards and remaining units of the old army were swept aside by the Germans at Narva, making it increasingly obvious that a more centralised and disciplined force would be necessary if the revolution was to survive. It was a contradictory task; to reinstitute discipline and build the army from above at a time when sections of the old army were still moving away from all those elements of its past life. Unsurprisingly, Trotsky's strategy—the construction of a regular standing army, the recruitment of officers from the tsarist army as 'military specialists', the dispersal of the soldiers' committees and the absorption of the Red Guards into the Red Army—provoked anger and distrust among many. The idea of a centralised army went against the grain of a revolutionary movement, and there was intense hostility from the rank and file towards the old officers. The use of 'military specialists' was obviously problematic, but efforts were made to avoid unpopular appointments, as Ilyin-Zhenevsky, a Bolshevik in the Petrograd Military Commissariat at the time, describes: 'We compiled a list of all the former officers who wished to serve in the Red Army and published this...During a period of ten days every citizen...had the right to object to the proposed appointment of any of these former officers'.[63]

The necessity for such an army was a step away from the socialist ideal of armed workers as a defence force, but the army did not revert to the nature of its tsarist predecessor. The army had to be not simply a military machine but a political force. Organised on a class basis, it provoked a 'frenzied howl of indignation from the bourgeois press',[64] which denounced the disorganisation and chaotic nature of the early army. Yet one former tsarist general contrasted the new army with the old army as it had disintegrated: 'Outwardly, the two things may seem identical—untidy dress, lack of respect for rank, careless performance of military duties—but *that* was the disorderliness of an order that had broken down, whereas *this* is the disorderliness of a structure that has not yet been put together. *There* one smelt decay, one tasted death: *here* we have the chaos of a new, clumsy process of construction and of uncompleted, not yet finally established forms'.[65]

Careful to preserve the revolutionary character of the army and to keep a tight grip on the military apparatus, each army commander was matched by political commissars drawn from socialist and anarchist organisations. Every army—there were 16 at the height of the war—had a Revolutionary Military Council (political department) usually consisting of at least two commissars who worked alongside the military commander, countersigning every order. The political commissar was 'the direct representative of the soviet power in the army'.[66]

The Red Army faced a powerful enemy. In the course of the summer of 1918, while the Czechoslovaks and KOMUCH were sweeping through Siberia, the White Volunteer Army was building its strength to 35,000-40,000 conscripted men, 86 field guns and 3 million roubles stolen from the Kuban peasants. By August the Whites had taken Siberia, the middle Volga and a large part of the Urals, and the workers' state faced a force stronger, better trained and better equipped than itself. As Chamberlin writes, 'The clash with the Czechoslovaks and the upsurge of Russian counter-revolution which accompanied it placed the Bolshevik leaders before a grim alternative: to create without too much delay an army that would fight and obey orders instead of debating them, or to go down in a welter of sanguinary defeat and fierce revenge on the part of the classes which they had driven from property and power'.[67]

With full scale civil war now upon them the Bolsheviks had no choice but to mobilise wider numbers. Conscription began in working class areas and the areas most at threat. Almost immediately it was clear that successful mobilisation went hand in hand with ensuring the cities had food supplies. Protests at the call-up were overwhelmingly linked to hunger—it was a military as well as a political imperative to ensure the army and the cities were fed.

Hunger notwithstanding, the majority of workers in Moscow and Petrograd responded. 'At the tables where the conscripts were registered long queues soon formed. But there was no uproar, no commotion. We felt that the workers were conscious of the importance of the duty they were performing,' records Ilyin-Zhenevsky.[68] The army grew from 331,000 in August 1918 to between 600,000 and 800,000. The actual numbers of those fighting in the major battles of the civil war were small by the standards of the First World War. Either side fought with at the most 100,000-150,000 in any one battle, the Whites numbering just 600,000 distributed over four fronts at their height in the summer of 1919. But with better equipment and trained leadership they could defeat the Reds if the latter had only equal numbers. And from virtually nothing, Ilyin-Zhenevsky testifies, 'We built, imperceptibly, stone upon stone, a new armed force for our republic. Just as a weakened and wounded animal puts on fresh fur as it recovers, so we covered ourselves with bayonets and came to look increasingly formidable to our opponents. The blood began to flow faster through our veins'.[69]

The military situation was seriously exacerbated by the LSR uprising in Moscow and Muraviev's mutiny. Significant numbers of LSRs were in high positions in the army, so the July events led to a wide call-up of members of the Communist Party (as the Bolsheviks were called from

March 1919) to strengthen the political composition of the army. The CP built itself organically into the army. By October 1919 there were 180,000 CP members in the army, rising to 278,000 in August 1920. Large numbers of workers who joined the party in the course of the war joined the army: 'According to official figures for Moscow workers some 70 percent of 20-24 year olds, 55 percent in the 25-29 age group and 35 percent of 30-35 year olds joined the Red Army'.[70] They were the political backbone of the army: their role as organisers of the army and of local revolts in White held areas was absolutely crucial—the revolutionaries made up the nervous system of the army.

The political departments were central in raising the political and cultural consciousness of the army. Half a million soldiers joined the party during the war, and the army was fighting a battle to make revolutionaries out of as many as possible. To this end, despite strained resources, the political departments poured out pamphlets, newspapers, posters and leaflets, and set up reading courses and mobile libraries to combat illiteracy so the soldiers could read reports from the other fronts and take active part in the debates arising in the new state. By the spring of 1919 reading and writing were taught daily. By the end of 1920 there were 3,000 Red Army schools, 60 amateur theatres, and libraries with reading rooms in every soldiers' club. The commitment to political education in the army is summed up in the first emblem of the army: the hammer and sickle with a rifle and a book. As Trotsky wrote in his autobiography, 'For us, the tasks of education in socialism were closely integrated with those of fighting. Ideas that enter the mind under fire remain there securely and forever'.[71]

John Reed attested to the atmosphere in the schools:

> One of these old professors gave an address on 'The Art of War' in which he glorified militarism... Podvoisky, representative of the Communist Party and of the Commissariat of War, immediately sprang to his feet. 'Comrade students!' he cried. 'I object to the spirit of the last speech. True, it is necessary to learn the art of war, but only in order that war may disappear forever. The Red Army is an army of peace. Our badge, our red star with the plough and hammer, shows what is our purpose—construction, not destruction. We do not make professional soldiers—we do not want them in our Red Army. So soon as we have crushed the counter-revolution—so soon as international revolution has put an end forever to imperialism, then shall we throw away our guns and swords, then shall frontiers be abolished, and we shall forget the art of war'.[72]

Building an army in a country already devastated by war was not an easy task. Desertion was a chronic problem for all the forces in the civil war. In the Red Army it is a factor that many historians cite to illustrate the tenuous nature of loyalty to the Soviet government. Many did desert—1,761,105 in 1919, the year with the highest figures—but numbers tell us nothing about motivations for desertion. Desertion figures include those who did not respond to the call-up. The Red Army specialist on desertion, Olikov, cites this figure at 75 percent for 1919, with 18-20 percent deserting on the way to the front, and only 5-7 percent deserting from combat units. These figures can be compared to the sign-up rate for KOMUCH in 1918 (30,000 from a population of 12 million) and the fact that the White armies were also dogged by lack of reinforcements.

Physical conditions, which were awful, were the main cause of desertion, although in some cases soldiers deserted *to* the front, where the food and supplies were better! Von Hagen points to a 1918 study showing that large numbers were deserting 'not because they were implacable enemies of the revolution, but simply because they were not receiving their rations. Many of these soldiers would return, after a few days absence, with a supply of bread'.[73]

And by 1919 when the majority in the army were peasants, there were seasonal desertions—soldiers would fight in the winter and harvest in the summer, especially if the front was close to home. This is a feature which is used to point to opposition among the peasantry to the Bolsheviks, but which could equally demonstrate a high level of commitment among soldiers. The predicament of the peasantry was addressed by the Bolsheviks through subsidies and tax exemptions for those who were unable to make the harvest. Such measures helped to break the mass desertions and the figure never again reached the same heights.

Although desertion was treated as a very serious crime, the 'draconian' discipline of the Bolsheviks was not as ruthless as we are led to believe. In the second half of 1919—when the Soviet government faced its most serious threat—612 deserters were executed out of 1,426,729. That represents one execution for every 2,331 deserters. Compare this to the figures for the British army during the First World War, where 278 executions took place out of 2,094 soldiers charged with desertion, quitting their posts or absence. Although the overall figure is lower, the proportion is higher—one in seven deserters were executed. The British army also confined its executions almost exclusively to the infantry—only three officers were executed for anything—while in the Red Army commissars and commanders were held responsible if their soldiers deserted or retreated. In the main desertion was punished with fines, the confiscation of property and work in the rear units. The vast majority of Russian deserters also returned to the army voluntarily when promised immunity from punishment.[74]

As a mass phenomenon, desertion was met with material aid to soldiers and their families, an expansion of political education and the promotion of workers and peasants to redress the balance within the army—so that by the end of the civil war only 34 percent of commanders were military specialists, and over 65,000 workers, peasants and Communists had taken their places. The regiments and brigades with the highest number of party members were almost uniformly those in which morale was highest. One report from the 2nd Brigade on the Southern Front in summer 1919 states that 'conscripts are extremely unreliable and their morale is bad. There are deserters.' The proposed solution was not repression:'It is essential that a large number of political workers shall be sent to be appointed as political commissars to carry out party work'.[75]

The attitude of the Bolsheviks towards desertion was, like every aspect of the army, integrated into an understanding of its social roots. Trotsky argued that every regiment and unit of the army was made up of a minority of committed and self sacrificing men, a minority of demoralised and hostile soldiers, and 'between these two minorities is a large middle group, the undecided, the vacillating. And when the better elements have been lost in fighting or shoved aside, and the skulkers and enemies get the upper hand, the unit goes to pieces. In such cases the large middle group do not know whom to follow and, in the moment of danger, succumb to panic'.[76] Repression against this vast majority would only drive a wedge between the revolution and its soldiers. The Red Army response—to provide new leaders and revolutionary education— served the dual purpose of raising morale and developing revolutionary consciousness among greater numbers.

This approach was not matched in either the People's Army or among the White armies. Under KOMUCH, wholesale desertions were met with repression: 'Peasant leaders were publicly flogged and hanged, hostages were taken to force the deserters out of hiding, and whole villages were burned to the ground when soldiers failed to give themselves up'.[77] Denikin's authorities in Rostov were 'continually publishing lists of deserting Cossacks, along with the number of lashes which were to be inflicted on them'.[78] Deserters often formed partisan bands to fight the White regime: 'So bitter was the antagonism aroused by many features of Denikin's policy and by many acts of his local administrators that efforts to carry out mobilisations in the Ukraine were more apt to produce rebellions and new "internal fronts" than reliable recruits'.[79]

Although much is made of mass peasant desertions and the relative weakness of Communist roots in the peasantry, it is clear, as Read admits, that the peasantry:

In the final analysis, preferred the arbitrary and oppressive Soviet institutions to the return of the Whites... Despite difficulties they did supply recruits. Seventy seven percent of the 4 million strong Red Army was made up of peasant conscripts in 1920. They did give large quantities of grain to supply the needs of the army and a proportion of what the city needed, although they received next to nothing in exchange. Even more significantly, there was nowhere in the entire empire where significant numbers of peasants supported the Whites.[80]

1919—the greatest danger

The first point at which the new army decisively checked the White forces was at Sviazhsk, a small town near Kazan on the Eastern Front, which was held by Czechoslovak troops in August 1918. When Trotsky arrived the scene that greeted him was one of despair and disorder among the troops. As he wrote later, 'The earth itself was seized by panic... Everything was breaking in pieces; there was no longer any firm point. The situation seemed hopeless'.[81] Within a few weeks Trotsky had transformed an incoherent collection of frightened and demoralised men into a serious fighting force—the backbone of the Fifth Army. Historians often view this achievement as resting purely on repression, but repression was not the deciding factor. As Trotsky wrote, 'Armies are not built on fear. The tsar's army fell apart not because of any lack of reprisals... The strongest cement in the new army was the ideas of the October Revolution'.[82] And the cement was provided on Trotsky's train—two engines carrying a printing press, telegraph and radio stations, its own generator, library and garage—in which he lived virtually constantly for two and a half years, travelling from front to front providing ceaseless propaganda, argument and pressure on the troops.

Trotsky's efforts bore fruit when the Fifth Army recaptured Kazan in September 1918. By now the Red Army had a 70,000 strong force on the Eastern Front, strengthened by an influx of party members, and it retook Simbirsk and Samara from the KOMUCH forces by October. White forces deserted in large numbers, as demoralised as the Reds had been two months earlier.

In November 1918 the German Revolution broke out, sweeping aside the monarchy and offering to fulfil the hopes of internationalism. Ilyin-Zhenevsky heard the news in a theatre: 'The announcement was met with a kind of roar, and frenzied applause shook the theatre for several minutes. There was noise and movement everywhere. One wanted to talk and talk endlessly. Here it was, it had come, support from the proletariat of Western Europe'.[83] But the prospect of German withdrawal from Russia also signalled the peril of Allied invasion. Lenin argued, 'First, we were never so near to international proletarian revolution as we are now. Second, we were never in a more dangerous position than at the present time'.[84]

The Whites saw in the German collapse the potential of substantial Allied aid for their cause and, in possession of the West Kuban at the end of 1918, Denikin pushed south and east towards the Caucasus mountains and the Caspian Sea, where his forces took Stavropol from the Taman Red Army. The Whites broke through the Red lines held by the 11th Army in January 1919. By February the North Caucasus Red Army no longer existed. The Whites took 50,000 prisoners, along with weapons and stores, and the Red troops who had avoided capture fled across the desert to Astrakhan, the 11th army alone losing 25,000 to typhus on the way. On the Eastern Front, Kolchak had taken the city of Perm in December 1918 and moved further west to take Ufa in the early months of 1919 before being driven back across the Urals in April and out of Siberia by the end of the year, his 400,000 strong force decimated by desertions and partisan fighting at his rear.

In June 1919 Denikin pushed north from the Don taking Kharkov, Ekaterinoslav and Tsaritsyn with the aid of British tanks and volunteers. From his new base at Tsaritsyn (subsequently Stalingrad), Denikin issued the Moscow Directive, intended to be a three pronged attack on the heart of Soviet power. The Whites eventually reached Orel, barely 250 miles from Moscow. The six months of fighting which ensued were bitter, and the privations borne by the population were devastating. John Reed wrote:

> The winter was horrible beyond imagination. No one will ever know what Russia went through. Transport at times almost ceased... There was, and is, grain enough in the provincial storehouses to feed the whole country well for two years, but it cannot be transported. For weeks together Petrograd was without bread. So with fuel—so with raw materials. Denikin's army held the Don coal mines and the oil wells of Grozny and Baku... In the great cities like Moscow and Petrograd the result was appalling. In some houses there was no heat at all the whole winter. People froze to death in their rooms... Ghastly things happened. Trains full of people travelling in remote provinces broke down between stations and the passengers starved and froze to death.[85]

The Whites had problems of their own. Stretched out over 1,000 miles of front with few reserves, with the same problems of partisan revolt in the rear and a lack of popular support that had tormented Kolchak, they steadily lost ground at Orel. The capture of Voronezh by the Red cavalry marked the turning point on the Southern Front. By the end of November Denikin's army was collapsing, carrying out horrendous pogroms against Jews in the Ukraine as it retreated.

At the height of the fighting on the Southern Front, the White general Yudenitch, a man described by Victor Serge as 'the perfect hangman', launched an attack on Petrograd from his base in Estonia. Unable to divert troops from the fight against Denikin, the defence of Petrograd was undertaken by the population of the revolution's birthplace. Trotsky rushed to Petrograd to take charge. He strengthened the 7th Army defending the city and prepared the workers for house to house fighting if necessary. Serge witnessed the events:

> In four days assistance has come from all parts of Russia. Zinoviev's radio telegram, which simply said, 'Petrograd is in danger!' has evoked responses from all over. Supply trains from all over the country have come—without waiting for special instructions—to unload their stocks of food at the Nicholas Station... The whole of Petrograd gives an impression of intense labour...barricades are springing out of the earth...the trenches are ready...a few metres in front, working women are stretching out barbed wire.[86]

The city was ready, but did not need to fight. The Red lines held, and Yudenitch was driven back to the outskirts at the end of October and finally dispatched in November. The last remaining White forces escaped to the Crimea, now commanded by General Wrangel.

In the belief that the war was over, the Bolsheviks moved to demobilise large parts of the Red Army at the end of 1919. The domestic situation was one of deep crisis. The civilian population suffered appalling deprivation—chronic malnutrition, epidemics and cold killed thousands. Sanitation was minimal. Patients froze to death in hospital beds. Red Army units were used as labour armies to rebuild the rail network and attempt to repair Russia's shattered infrastructure.

However, after only three months of respite, in April and May 1920 Polish troops under Pilsudski invaded Lithuania and east Galicia, which was part of independent Ukraine under the nationalist leader Petliura. Together with Petliura's partisans, and backed by the French, the 738,000 strong Polish army struck the Red Army's South Western Front. Exhausted, with 30 percent of the army suffering from typhus, the Soviet government launched another recruitment drive to counter the threat.

Initially successful at driving back the Polish army, the Red Army went further and launched an attack on Warsaw driven by the belief that Polish workers would rise up against Pilsudski. Whatever the merits of the strategy militarily, it was disastrous politically. Marching on Warsaw with the aim of bringing the revolution to Poland, the army was repulsed, with no sign of a workers' uprising to welcome them. Trotsky relates that the extent of revolutionary feeling among workers in Poland was not clear to the Soviet leadership. In the event, he argued, the opportunities to turn the war from one of defence to an offensive revolutionary war failed because the movement in Poland had not matured by the time the Red Army entered Warsaw: 'Where the action of armies is measured in days and weeks, the movement of the masses is usually reckoned in months and years. If this difference in tempo is not taken fully into account, the gears of war will only break the teeth of the revolutionary gears instead of setting them in motion'.[87] The invasion of Poland is seen as proof that the Bolsheviks always planned to export 'socialism' by force. Clearly, the attempt to spread the revolution forcibly was a mistaken attempt at a short cut to workers' power in Poland—but it was not a premonition of Stalin's imposed 'socialism'.

There is a world of difference between invading a country in the hope of stimulating revolution, and doing so in order to crush it, as Stalinist Russia did in Hungary 1956, for example. The overwhelming desire of the Bolsheviks at this point, and since 1917, was the internationalisation of the revolution and the establishment of genuine workers' democratic socialism.

In addition the leadership of the Bolsheviks were not united on the question of Poland. Trotsky had argued against Lenin, unhappy with the plan of taking revolution to the Polish working class 'at the point of a bayonet'. But rather than expressing Lenin's desire for dictatorship, the invasion of Poland illustrates what is the central thesis of this article— the extent to which the Bolsheviks were affected by imperatives imposed by three years of war in which the entire society had been geared to the war effort, and were desperate to end their own isolation. In the absence of revolution elsewhere the leadership knew very well that the Russian Revolution could not survive. The attempt to stimulate revolution by sheer will was a failure, but flowed from the predicament in which they were caught.

The war with Poland also provided the remnants of the White armies a final gasp. With all eyes to the West, Wrangel seized his chance to push out of the Crimea—now the last refuge of hundreds of thousands of White supporters—to the Northern Tauride and into the Kuban. It was a last ditch attempt to rally support which foundered on the same rock of repressive land legislation and Greater Russian nationalism that had contributed to the failures of Kolchak and Denikin before him. On the third anniversary of the revolution the Red Army, having driven Wrangel back to the Crimea, routed his army and he was forced to evacuate 145,000 White supporters in French and British warships.

Why the Whites lost

Despite the enormous privations of the war years the Bolsheviks succeeded in defeating the vast array of forces against them. For Richard Pipes, who is ready to ascribe the start of the war to Bolshevik ideology, the 'decisive factors' in the outcome of the war 'were of an objective nature'.[88] By objective, he is referring to the geographic size of Russia, Bolshevik control of an area with a larger population, and the greater supply of weaponry on the Red side.

It is unquestionably true that the Bolsheviks were at their strongest in the urban heartlands, relatively protected from direct Allied intervention into the north, Siberia and the Crimea. The sheer size of the country and the location of the revolution's enemies on its peripheries, where they had been driven in the first months of the war, initially allowed the Soviet government time to build an army. However, the enormous distances also posed huge problems in the movement and supply of troops—with constantly moving fronts the Red Army had to spread itself over a vast area in order to protect the centre. The dislocation of transport, including Allied control of the Trans-Siberian Railway and the continual fighting in the Volga region, negated many of the potential advantages of being at the centre of a rail network, making it difficult to move supplies and necessitating the requisitioning of food by frontline soldiers.

According to Pipes's figures, the Bolsheviks controlled the areas with the highest concentration of war industries, with 46.3 percent in Moscow and Petrograd, 38.6 percent in the White-occupied Urals and the Ukraine,and 25.1 percent in Poland and areas under occupation by the Germans in the west. By Pipes's own admission, however, this dubious 'advantage' was academic, as 'in 1918 Russian defence industries had virtually stopped functioning' and did not start again until the end of that year.[89] Even when production resumed there were huge problems in supplying the army. The massive decline in industrial production, coupled with disrupted transport and separation from areas containing raw materials, meant the Bolsheviks were relying on stocks from the tsarist army. Although there *were* large stocks (2.5 million rifles, 12,000 field guns, 2.8 million artillery shells), Trotsky described the tsarist legacy as chaotic: 'Of some things there was too much, of others too little, and, besides, we did not know just what we possessed.'

The Allied blockade further aggravated the situation, preventing any military supplies reaching the Bolsheviks from abroad—a problem the Whites did not suffer from. As a result, one report from the Fifth Army on the Eastern Front states that '50 percent of the Red Army men have no footwear, greatcoats or underclothes. As the cold nights set in, illnesses caused by the cold are increasing every day'.[90] Even when supplies were sent they did not always reach the fronts: 'By the summer of 1919 there was an acute shortage of bullets; the armies on the Southern Front, where the fighting at this time was especially severe, were obliged to lead a hand to mouth existence, with stocks of bullets which would not have been regarded as sufficient for a regiment in a single day of heavy fighting during the First World War'.[91]

In 1920, *after* war production had been revived, Trotsky could write, 'We had no reserves. Every rifle, every cartridge, every pair of boots was despatched, straight from the machine or the lathe that produced it, to the front.' The progress of the Red Army was often badly affected: 'The supply of munitions was always as taut as a string. Sometimes the string would break and then we lost men and territory'.[92]

Objective circumstances alone, therefore, did not mean that the victory of the Red Army was a foregone conclusion. Had the Bolsheviks not enjoyed greater political support than their enemies the advantages provided by their objective circumstances would have been much less decisive. Equally, factors which are deemed to be 'objective' on the White side—difficulties with recruitment, a dependence on unreliable allies like the Cossacks, the vacillations of the Allied powers and the lack of co-operation between armies—are all coloured by the political choices that they and other groups in society made.

The White regimes returned the land to the landowners and the factories to the owners, denied trade union rights to workers, and were characterised by corruption, decadence, speculation and bitter repression of the population. The class in whose name the Whites fought was weak and crumbling, and was savagely lashing out in its decay. Within industrial centres controlled by Whites a reign of terror against workers was routine. In the Donbass, one in ten workers were shot if coal production fell, and 'some workers were shot for simply being workers under the slogan, 'Death to callused hands'.[93]

Both Kolchak and Denikin saw their mission as the restoration of a 'great and undivided Russia', a policy which alienated their potential allies among the Cossacks—many of whom refused to fight in the last battles of the civil war. Much of the population under Denikin's rule consisted of non-Russians who had no interest in returning to the oppression of the tsarist 'prison house of nations'.

Kolchak's refusal to countenance independence for Finland resulted in a denial of Finnish support to Yudenitch in his march on Petrograd in winter 1919.

The White regimes failed to mobilise large numbers of people in their support. The classes that identified with them—the officers, landowners, factory owners, middle class and intelligentsia—were certainly sufficient for the task of building a strong army and attracting outside aid, but the wider uprisings against the Bolsheviks that they hoped for did not materialise. However much Denikin tried to base the Whites' 'ideology on simple, incontestable national symbols', by his own admission, 'This proved extraordinarily difficult. "Politics" burst into our work. It burst spontaneously also into the life of the army'.[94]

Characterised by one of Kolchak's generals as, 'In the army, decay; in the staff, ignorance and incompetence; in the government, moral rot, disagreement and intrigues of ambitious egotists; in the country, uprising and anarchy; in public life, panic, selfishness, bribes and all sorts of scoundrelism',[95] the White regime at Omsk was a brutal and arbitrary dictatorship. It liquidated the trade unions and meted out savage reprisals against peasants who sheltered partisans—reprisals which inflamed the population and pushed many towards Bolshevism. When Omsk was taken by the Red Army in November 1919, it was with the willing participation of large numbers of peasant recruits. In many Siberian towns workers overthrew the Kolchak government before the Red troops arrived. In Irkutsk a Political Centre was established to govern in place of the Whites, which in turn was replaced by a mainly Bolshevik revolutionary committee installed by the workers in January 1920, to whom Kolchak was delivered after his capture.

The Whites lost because they were less popular among the majority classes in Russia, a factor which hindered their military abilities once it became necessary to build a large conscript army. As Lenin pointed out in July 1919, 'A general mobilisation will finish Denikin off, just as it finished off Kolchak. So long as his army was a class one, consisting only of volunteers of an anti-socialist character, it was strong and reliable...but the greater the size of his army, the less class conscious it was, and the weaker it became'.[96] This was precisely what happened—revolts at the rear of Denikin's army forced him to send troops back from the front, and having to conscript a hostile population increased the difficulties, weakening his ability to push forward to Moscow.

Another 'objective' factor cited by Pipes is the 'weakly developed sense of patriotism among the Russian population',[97] a position which dovetails with the Menshevik view of the time of the Russian people as immature, unruly masses with no sense of what the revolution and war were about. But patriotism had not been weakly developed at the outbreak of the First World War—although 1 million deserters had been expected, all but a few thousand out of 15 million accepted the call-up. What took place subsequently was the breakdown of nationalism and allegiance to the old ruling class, and a huge step forward in the collective consciousness. The lack of support for the Whites would be more accurately attributed to the generalised shift in attitudes *beyond* Russian nationalism towards self rule and national freedom, a goal that the

Bolshevik Party embodied and the Whites threatened to extinguish.

Pipes argues that the Bolshevik claim to enjoy mass support is 'entirely inapplicable' where 'it is secured and maintained by force'.[98] Clearly, repression was a feature of the civil war. To overthrow the old ruling class and to wage war against it could not be other than authoritarian and repressive. Frederick Engels wrote, 'A revolution is certainly the most authoritarian thing there is; it is the act whereby one part of the population imposes its will upon the other part by means of rifles, bayonets and cannon—authoritarian means, if such there be at all'.[99] He was pointing to the cold reality that in order to be successful the revolution must be prepared to be ruthless to its enemies, internal and external.

However, repression was not the deciding factor in the Bolsheviks' hold on power. The Russian working class and peasantry had made a revolution to end one war and had walked away from the trenches despite threats of repression. It defies logic that the Bolsheviks could have built and maintained an army of 3 million and mobilised people to fight again through force alone. The best form of recruitment was inspiration. Whereas the Whites could only offer the old world or worse, the Bolsheviks had—despite the hardships—taken power from the exploiters, given land to the peasants and established workers' control. Political choices cannot simply be reduced to responses to 'objective' circumstances. Those who supported the Bolsheviks were defending the gains of the revolution in order to extend them, and were therefore motivated by much more positive emotions than fear.

This is a fact that may elude today's historians, but it did not escape the notice of the Whites. One of their spies in Petrograd in 1919 reported that 'the worker elements, at least a large section of them, are still Bolshevik inclined... Psychologically, they identify the present with equality and Soviet power and the Whites with the old regime and its scorn for the masses'.[100] At the height of Kolchak's drive to the west in spring 1919 the workers of Orenburg organised the defence of their town and prevented its capture by the Whites, and when Denikin threatened Tula, the key armaments base for the Reds, a quarter of a million deserters flooded back to the Red Army from Orel and Moscow alone. The price of White victory would have been the crushing of the gains of October, and the majority of the population did not want tsarism or dictatorship.

In fact, had the Whites won, the alternative would have been far worse than the restoration of the old regime. As the war swept away the middle ground, the alternative was increasingly clear. As one of Kolchak's generals, Šakharov, boasted from exile in Germany after Mussolini's rise to power, 'The White movement was in essence the first manifestation of fascism'.[101]

The imperialist powers were also aware of the depth of Bolshevik support. A memo to the British war cabinet in July 1919 illustrates the point: 'It is impossible to account for the stability of the Bolshevik government by terrorism alone... When the Bolshevik fortunes seemed to be at the lowest ebb, a most vigorous offensive was launched before which the Kolchak forces are still in retreat. No terrorism, not even long suffering acquiescence, but something approaching enthusiasm is necessary for this. We must admit then that the present Russian government is accepted by the bulk of the Russian people'.[102]

The recent debate

In the last few years the debate on the Russian Revolution has moved on. The collapse of Stalinism has led to a strengthening of the position of conservative historians like Richard Pipes that the October Revolution was a coup, that totalitarianism was a feature of the Bolshevik Party from the beginning, and that the civil war enabled the fulfilment of Bolshevik aims of dictatorship.

Though written in the mid-1970s, social historian Roger Pethybridge's statement, 'The violence of the civil war was a result of Lenin's seizure of power without a general mandate',[103] finds its echo in Evan Mawdsley's more recent offering: 'Both the civil war and Stalinism were likely consequences of the seizure of power'.[104] Another approach to the revolution and its aftermath can be observed in accounts based on social history, on the perspective of the working class and the peasantry, but which come to conclusions which mirror the conservative approach. Orlando Figes' book, *A People's Tragedy*, concludes that the outcome of the revolution was inevitable, as the population was too backward and immature to prevent the Bolsheviks from using the revolution for their own ends.

These two strands of history writing on Russia are in part driven by a disillusionment in the revolutionary project in the wake of Stalinism's collapse. However, both the resurgence of the Cold War conservative attitudes and the emergence of pessimistic, though more liberal, accounts are linked to weaknesses in the approach of genuine social historians in the last two decades.[105] Those historians, including Diane Koenker, William Rosenberg, Daniel Kaiser and Steve Smith, wrote good accounts which were generally sympathetic to the revolutionary project. However, a lack of clarity about the nature of the Soviet Union following Stalin's rise to power has led to generalised confusion since the collapse of Stalinism. Sheila Fitzpatrick has summed this up: 'All serious scholars of the former Soviet Union are undergoing a process of conceptual readjustment, just as physicists and biologists would be when confronted by a sudden influx of new experimental data, not to mention a new regime of experimentation'.[106]

The history from below approach taken by some of these historians also suffered from its focus on the popular movement to the exclusion of other class forces in Russian society—a weakness which contributes to a belief that the Bolsheviks' options in the civil war period were solely determined by the demands and aspirations of the workers and peasants, and not also shaped by the role of other classes both in Russia and abroad.

The question of ideology and class consciousness is also important here. While the history from below approach accepts there was support from the popular movement for the Bolsheviks, it tends to see the connection as coincidental, that workers' political ideas were a direct result of the social changes taking place, so they moved away from the Bolsheviks as social circumstances changed. A rounded analysis of the politics of the civil war, however, must take into account not only the impact of social circumstances on political ideas and party allegiance but also the way in which the process of revolution transformed politics on a huge scale, and how resilient those ideas were in the civil war period. Without understanding the extent to which conceptions about society shifted it is impossible to fully understand how the civil war was fought, let alone won. As Mike Haynes has written, not integrating the role of politics into social history results in historians taking a position which:

> ...both sees divergence [between the Bolsheviks and the popular movement] *as inevitable and which comes close to endorsing the position argued by many Mensheviks after October 1917...to the effect that the Bolsheviks were riding the crest of a temporary wave and should have had the good sense to realise that it could not last and therefore refused power. This also, of course, absolves the other parties of any responsibility for the subsequent development of the revolution and diminishes an analysis of the choices that they made.*[107]

The weaknesses of social history can be seen in Christopher Read's book *From Tsar to Soviets*. Seeking to relocate the popular movement at the heart of the revolution and the civil war, Read nonetheless falls into an acceptance of the Lenin-Stalin link, claiming that it was the 'Bolsheviks, not the counter-revolution, who suppressed the popular movement—during the civil war, at the time of Tambov and Kronstadt and, eventually, through collectivisation and the Great Terror which seemed to have extirpated it for good'.[108]

The civil war period highlights the interrelation of politics and material circumstances: the revolutionary process transformed political ideas, and political imperatives shaped economic and military policy. However, an analysis which understands the relative independence of consciousness loses its power if ideology is then seen as *the* motor for historical change.

So Read, in his insistence that 'ironically a, possibly the, key reason for the failure of the "dream scenario" did not lie with the revolution's enemies on the right...but from its Bolshevik "friends",'[109] reaches a conclusion akin to the conservative view that Bolshevik ideology, not material circumstances, lay at the root of the revolution's degeneration.

The legacy

The revolution was victorious in the civil war, but at an enormous cost.

The civil war shattered industrial production: total industrial output fell to 18 percent of its already extremely low pre-war levels. In 1920 production of pig iron was a mere 2.4 percent of its pre-war figure, the corresponding figure for coal was 27 percent, for sugar 6.7 percent, for electrical engineering machinery 5.4 percent and for cotton goods 5.1 percent.[110]

The foreign blockade reduced imports and exports to a tiny fraction of their 1917 figures, resulting in widespread hunger and disease. At the end of the war 350,000 were dead in battle and 450,000 had died of disease. Between the end of 1918 and the end of 1920 hunger, cold and disease had killed 9 million people—typhus killed one million in 1920 alone. The war effort had 'plundered all of Russia' and destroyed much of its industry. Fan belts were torn out of machinery in the factories to make boots for the army; 64 of the largest factories in Petrograd were forced to close for lack of fuel. For economic historian Kritsman, 'Such a fall of the productive forces...of a huge society of 100 million people...is unexampled in the history of mankind'.[111] It is difficult to express the full magnitude of such horror on Russian society. Read sums this up well: 'Terms like crisis and collapse are used frequently today, even to describe situations where economic growth falls below 2 percent. There is no word of strong enough force to use when one comes to the situation of Russia in these years'.[112]

The impact of the war was not solely economic. All the major classes underwent enormous upheaval:

> Russia's social structure had been not merely overturned; it was smashed and destroyed. The social classes which had so implacably and furiously wrestled with one another in the civil war were all, with the partial exception of the peasantry, either exhausted and prostrate or pulverised. The landed gentry had perished in their burning mansions and on the battlefields of the civil war; survivors escaped abroad with remnants of the White armies which scattered to the winds. Of the bourgeoisie, never very numerous or politically confident, many had also perished or emigrated. Those who saved their skins...were merely the wreckage of their class'.[113]

Though victorious against its class enemies, the working class was also devastated. In Russia as a whole it was reduced to 43 percent of its former number. The population of Petrograd fell from 2.4 million in 1917 to 574,000 in 1920—cut by 76 percent from its October 1917 figure. Those who worked in the factories were often not the same workers who had made the revolution. The army had drained the urban centres dry of the most militant workers, who were replaced in the factories by peasants often lacking the same revolutionary commitment. By the end of the war, the Bolsheviks were ruling in the name of a class which was at best a shadow of its former self: 'The world's first proletarian government had to watch the class on which it claimed to be based diminish from its already weak minority position'.[114]

Naturally, the party itself changed as the working class disintegrated. The distortions within the Bolsheviks were not ideologically motivated. A revolutionary party rests on its links and roots in the working class, learning from the class as well as leading. Without that class, the party becomes isolated—the blood supply necessary to maintain its health greatly reduced. In addition, as the crack troops of the Red Army, an estimated 50 percent of Communist Party members who fought in the civil war were killed, wounded or ill after major battles. The party branches outside the army were also hit hard by the war. The working class membership of the party eroded. In 1917 workers had made up 60 percent of the party; by 1920-1921 that had fallen to 41 percent, the bulk of whom worked for the state or the army rather than in the factories. Careerists joined in large numbers, further diluting the composition of the party. At the same time, the Soviet government was presiding over an increasingly hostile peasant majority. There were strikes in Petrograd, revolts in the countryside, and the garrison at Kronstadt mutinied in March 1921. Once the immediate enemies were defeated, the hardships the population had endured for three years became the cause of dramatic conflict with the goverment.

To understand the changes in the party it is essential to understand the impact of social degeneration and economic disaster on political principles and ideology. The gap between dreams and reality had widened dramatically in the course of the war, at times leading the Bolsheviks to extol the virtues of policies enacted from dire necessity. There were deep political shifts in the circumstances—it would have been incredible if there were not. But this does not mean that the rise of Stalinism was inevitably the result of Bolshevik politics, or that revolutionary Leninism contained the seeds of its own destruction. As Victor Serge put it, 'It is often said that the germ of all Stalinism was in Bolshevism at its beginning. Well, I have no objection. Only, Bolshevism also contained many other germs—a mass of other germs—and those who lived through the enthusiasm of the first years of the first victorious revolution ought not to forget it. To judge the living man by the death germs which the autopsy reveals in a corpse—and which he may have carried with him since his birth—is this very sensible?'[115]

Political will and the revolutionary impulse achieved miracles in the course of the civil war, in the context of appalling social conditions. But the Bolsheviks could not build a socialist society from sheer willpower. It is an incredible achievement on the Bolsheviks' part that they held out as long as they did, and it is testimony to the party's organisation and discipline, and the powerful impetus the revolution had given to creativity and commitment, that even as late as 1928, with Stalin's consolidation of power, he was forced to physically wipe out the last vestiges of it by murdering or exiling the old Bolsheviks.

It is to be regretted that so many historians, lacking clarity about the nature of the regime which finally beheaded the revolution, have given ground to the theory of an inevitable connection between revolutionary and Stalinist Russia. By locating the civil war period in its historical context, by attempting to draw out the relative weight of objective circumstances and ideology in the most dramatic period of the revolution's history, it is possible to counter those arguments with a more thorough understanding.

Fortunately, Stalinism is now dead, and in the context of the resulting ideological ferment, there is huge potential for a genuine reading of the Russian Revolution to gain wider currency, not as a history lesson but as a guide for revolutionaries today.

Notes

1 V P Butt, A B Murphy, N A Myshov and G R Swain (eds), *The Russian Civil War: Documents from the Soviet Archives* (Macmillan, 1996), pviii.
2 Quoted in A Callinicos, *The Revolutionary Ideas of Karl Marx* (Bookmarks, 1987), p99.
3 M Ferro, *October 1917* (Routledge, 1980), p161.
4 Ibid, p162.
5 Ibid, p164.
6 M Phillips Price, *Dispatches from the Russian Revolution* (Pluto, 1997), p83
7 C Read, *From Tsar to Soviets* (UCL, 1996), p191.
8 E Mawdsley, *The Russian Civil War* (Allen & Unwin, 1987), p22.
9 Ibid, p44.
10 The Socialist Revolutionary Party, with a mainly peasant base, had split into Left and Right in November 1917, with the Left joining a coalition government with the Bolsheviks.
11 V P Butt et al, op cit, p8.
12 O Figes, *A People's Tragedy* (Pimlico, 1996), p582.
13 V P Butt et al, op cit, p33.

14 M von Hagen, *The Soldier in the Proletarian Dictatorship* (Cornell University, 1990), p125.
15 V P Butt et al, op cit, pvii.
16 R Pipes, op cit, p63.
17 E Mawdsley, op cit, p43.
18 W Chamberlin, *The Russian Revolution*, vol 1 (Princeton, 1987), pp409-410.
19 Ibid, p411.
20 Quoted in V Serge, *Year One of the Russian Revolution* (Bookmarks, 1992), p187.
21 Ibid, p189.
22 M Phillips Price, *Dispatches from the Weimar Republic* (Pluto, 1999), p47.
23 E Mawdsley, op cit, p283.
24 V P Butt et al, op cit, p43.
25 R Pipes, op cit, p74.
26 Quoted ibid, p46.
27 J F C Fuller, *The Decisive Battles of the Western World* (Paladin, 1970), p403.
28 R Pipes, op cit, p12.
29 C Read, op cit, p184.
30 R Pipes, op cit, p74.
31 E Mawdsley, op cit, p283.
32 E H Carr, *The Bolshevik Revolution 1917-1923*, vol 2 (Pelican, 1971), p130.
33 R Pipes, op cit, p79.
34 Ibid, p79.
35 O Figes, op cit, p652.
36 W Chamberlin, op cit, vol 2, p170.
37 Ibid, p162.
38 J Reed, *Shaking the World: Revolutionary Journalism* (Bookmarks, 1998), p246.
39 E H Carr, op cit, p245.
40 E H Carr, op cit, p246.
41 Quoted in Pipes, op cit, p419.
42 Noted ibid, p419.
43 C Read, p292.
44 J Jacobson, *When the Soviet Union Entered World Politics* (University of California, 1994), p13.
45 W Chamberlin, op cit, vol 2, p171.
46 R Pipes, op cit, p6.
47 C Read, op cit, p193.
48 L Trotsky, *My Life* (Penguin, 1986), p411.
49 Quoted in E Wollenberg, *The Red Army* (New Park, 1978), p12.
50 W Chamberlin, op cit, vol 1, p425.
51 Ibid, p106.
52 M Haynes, 'Social History and the Russian Revolution', in *Essays on Historical Materialism* (Bookmarks, 1998), p69.
53 M Desai (ed), *Lenin's Economic Writings* (Lawrence & Wishart, 1989), p177-178.
54 C Read, op cit, p239.
55 E Mawdsley, op cit, p75.
56 Quoted in E Wollenberg, op cit, p12.
57 W Chamberlin, op cit, vol 1, p420.
58 Ibid.
59 M von Hagen, op cit, p334.
60 Quoted ibid, p5.
61 L Trotsky, *How the Revolution Armed: Military Writings* (New Park, 1979), vol 1, p4.
62 Ibid, p7.
63 A F Ilyin-Zhenevsky, *The Bolsheviks in Power* (New Park, 1984), p70.

64 Ibid, p14.
65 Quoted ibid, p34.
66 L Trotsky, *How the Revolution Armed*, op cit, p7.
67 W Chamberlin, op cit, vol 2, p23.
68 A F Ilyin-Zhenevsky, op cit, p118.
69 Ibid.
70 Quoted in C Read, op cit, p254.
71 L Trotsky, *My Life*, op cit, p449.
72 J Reed, op cit, p247.
73 Ibid, p46.
74 E Wollenberg, op cit, p43.
75 V P Butt et al, op cit, p98.
76 L Trotsky, *My Life*, op cit, p429.
77 O Figes, op cit, p583.
78 W Chamberlin, op cit, vol 2, p265.
79 Ibid.
80 C Read, op cit, p237.
81 Quoted in W Chamberlin, op cit, vol 2, p118.
82 L Trotsky, *My Life*, op cit, p427.
83 A F Ilyin-Zhenevsky, op cit, p128.
84 Quoted in W Chamberlin, op cit, vol 2, p121.
85 J Reed, op cit, p243.
86 V Serge, *Revolution in Danger* (Redwords, 1997), pp58-59.
87 L Trotsky, *My Life*, op cit, p476.
88 R Pipes, op cit, p9.
89 Ibid, p12.
90 V P Butt et al, op cit, p99.
91 W Chamberlin, op cit, vol 2, p35.
92 L Trotsky, *My Life*, op cit, p433.
93 O Figes, op cit, p665.
94 Quoted in R Pipes, op cit, p14.
95 Ibid, p195.
96 E Wollenberg, op cit, p98.
97 R Pipes, op cit, p135.
98 Ibid, p136.
99 F Engels, *On Authority*, quoted in M von Hagen, op cit, p13.
100 Quoted in O Figes, p674.
101 C Read, op cit, p198.
102 Quoted in R Pipes, op cit, p97.
103 R Pethybridge, *The Social Prelude to Stalinism* (Macmillan, 1977), p79.
104 E Mawdsley, op cit, p289.
105 I am indebted to Mike Haynes for my understanding of the current debates on the revolution. For a fuller and more knowledgable discussion see his 'Social History and the Russian Revolution", in *Essays on Historical Materialism*, op cit; 'The Debate on Popular Violence and the Popular Movement in the Russian Revolution', in *Historical Materialism* 2 (Summer 1998); and 'The Return of the Mob', in *Journal of Area Studies* 13, 1998.
106 S Fitzpatrick, 'Better To Bend the Stick too Far', *London Review of Books*, 4 February 1999.
107 M Haynes, 'The Return of the Mob', op cit.
108 C Read, op cit, p293.
109 Ibid, pp292-293.
110 See T Cliff, *Lenin*, vol 3, (Bookmarks, 1987), pp86-87.
111 Quoted in E Mawdsley, op cit, p288.

112   C Read, op cit, p192.
113   I Deutscher, *Trotsky*, vol 2 (Oxford University Press, 1987), p5.
114   C Read, op cit, p193.
115   Quoted in V Serge, *Memoirs of a Revolutionary* (Writers and Readers, 1984), pxv.

Reviewing the millennia

A review of C Harman, A People's History of the World (Bookmarks, 1999), £15.99

ROBIN BLACKBURN

Our culture is today prey to seemingly relentless commercialisation and dumbing down. Fortunately there are some counter-tendencies and one of those is the evidence of widespread interest in world history, anthropology and archaeology. While the bestseller lists are crammed with the likes of Jeffrey Archer, John Gray and Jilly Cooper, respectable sales can still be achieved by serious works of popularisation by authors like Richard Leakey or Stephen Jay Gould. When it comes to world history, writers like Jared Diamond and William McNeill can find hundreds of thousands of readers for books which offer a materialist perspective. Thus McNeill has surveyed the differential impact of disease in *Plagues and Peoples*, and more recently Jared Diamond's *Guns, Germs and Steel* has had great success. These works have their weaknesses, usually that of pursuing a valid insight further than it can go, missing vital aspects of the complex texture of human social relations. So McNeill has much to teach us concerning the impact of microbes; but while he does have a concept for the exploitative features of social structure, it is a rather simplistic one. Likewise Diamond offers an ecological explanation of why agricultural development flourished more consistently and cumulatively in Eurasia than Africa, which perhaps tries to explain too much but nevertheless at least poses the question in ways that provoke helpful argument. His thesis is that Africa's north-south succession of very different terrains—desert, savannah, tropical rainforest, veldt etc—greatly impeded the spread of domesticated plants and animals while Eurasia's lateral spread of somewhat more similar habitats facilitated it. While Diamond is able to elaborate his account in interesting ways, by the end of several hundred pages the danger of reductionism is palpable.

The serious concerns of such work contrast not only to the frivolities of 'infotainment', but also to the whimsy of the occult or the narrow and obtuse specialisms of academia. Evidently there is a popular thirst for authors who try to explain where we have come from and where we are going, and who confront the large questions without recourse to the supernatural. Socialist writers have always seen this as one of their essential tasks; the fact that *The Communist Manifesto* offers a compelling historical sketch as well as a vivid sense of what drives global development helps to explain its enduring appeal.

Chris Harman's *A People's History of the World* is a very welcome and largely successful attempt to produce a popular history of the human species, bringing out the interconnection between the development of modes of production on the one hand and class struggle on the other. The book is closer in spirit to *The Communist Manifesto* than to *Capital,* because of this interweaving of story and structure while taking into account a further century and a half of history and historiography. It is 729 pages long, with the last 150 years taking up just over half the space. But to put this another way, Harman still devotes 300 pages to events and developments prior to the industrial revolution. Early chapters cover the farming revolution, the urban revolution, and the rise of the early states and empires, drawing on the work of Jared Diamond as well as Gordon Childe's classic materialist studies in pre-history, updating Childe's account with the later findings of such scholars as Colin Renfrew and Charles Maizels.

Some topics could, perhaps, have received a bit more attention. It would have been interesting to have more on what Harman thinks about the new evidence concerning conditions of life in the first settled communities, or on the origins and spread of language, or on variations in family form and their link to the dynamic of different relations of production, or on the impact of nomad warriors on history. But given the book's already considerable length, it is clear that hard choices had to be made about coverage. And lest I imply that Harman is uninterested in cultural superstructures, I should add that he has chapters on the rise of Christianity and Islam. Indeed, I have the impression that he attributes too much importance to the intrinsic qualities of Christian ideology and too little to the fact that its decisive growth occurred after it had become the state religion of the Roman Empire.

Marxist accounts of world history have sometimes been accused of Eurocentrism but Harman makes an effort to give space to the fate of Asian empires, to the impact of Islam, to Africa and the Americas, and to resistance to slavery, racism and colonialism. If Europe still looms quite large in the story there is a reason for that—namely that the capitalism and imperialism which developed most strongly in Europe, and in the lands settled by Europeans, have dominated the world history of the last few centuries. Writers as diverse as Jack Goody and Andre Gunder Frank have recently been disposed to object that the dominance of European capitalism is a more recent and a more shallow phenomenon than Marxists have traditionally supposed. Some authors are now claiming that China was as developed as, or even more developed than, Europe as recently as 1800 and that it is likely to catch back up within the next 20 years or so.[1]

It is, perhaps, in the relative weight accorded to China's history that a certain residual Eurocentrism may be detected. Today more than a fifth of the world's people live in China and the last century and a half of that country's history has embraced an extraordinary sequence of events leading up to both the Communist seizure of power and a recent surge of economic development without parallel in the Third World. Harman devotes only two pages—and in substance really only two paragraphs—to the the crucial two decades between 1930 and 1950. The 19th century T'ai-p'ing Rebellion and the revolutionary struggles of the 1920s are properly dealt with, but little attempt is made to assess the overall significance of the last quarter century. Harman is prepared to allow that the Stalinist regime did, at terrible cost, modernise the Russian economy, but he does not essay a comparable balance sheet of China's development.

The long term perspective of macro-history can illuminate contemporary history in important ways. Thus awareness of the historical achievements of Chinese and Indian agriculture helps to explain different patterns of rural-urban relations in today's world. Thus in Africa migrant workers send back a stream of remittances to the villages from which they come; in much of Asia workers can be hired for less than the cost of their upkeep because they receive food from their villages.

Ensuring even and comprehensive coverage in a work such as this is extraordinarily difficult, especially if the aim is to keep the story going and to convey the overall sense of pattern and direction in human affairs. Without forcing the evidence Harman does usually succeed in conveying that sense of flow, as of some gigantic river, and in deftly identifying counter-eddies, the silting up of some channels and the opening of others. Popular struggles are recounted, but also the historical conditions which both favour and frustrate them. A good example here would be his account of the French Revolution and of the impact of Jacobinism outside France's borders in Britain and Ireland, in Italy and Germany, and in the Caribbean and Latin America.

The still-dominant national framework for the writing of history characteristically misses the way that events and ideas overspill national borders. Harman's account of the 20th century gains from the fact that he tries to see it whole. He rightly insists on the far-reaching and disastrous impact of the First World War, whose carnage and brutality did so much to make possible and probable (not, of course, inevitable) the subsequent rise of Stalinism and Nazism. A global perspective is needed, not only because this allows us to compare and contrast, but also because there are shared themes and common impulses.

This is a book about history and not a book about books. But from time to time Harman does allude to controversies and authorities so that it is not inappropriate to suggest that when he came to such a decisive watershed as the rise of capitalism he should have provided his readers with some signposts to the great controversies to which the study of this event has given rise. As it happens the work of Marxist writers—Maurice Dobb, Paul Sweezy, Eric Hobsbawm and Robert Brenner—has attracted what are widely acknowledged to be the central debates on 'the transition' and 'the crisis of the 17th century' so it would have been especially helpful for Harman to have addressed them more directly. However, the reader does glean that Harman is not persuaded by those whose single minded focus on the emergence of a capitalist calculus in north west Europe has led them to neglect material constraints and technology on the one hand, and Marx's own theses on 'primitive accumulation' and 'bourgeois revolution' on the other. When forced to choose, Harman is more concerned with understanding the connection of events than exploring the intricacies of structural logic, a very understandable preference for someone attempting to cover the whole span of history in a single book.

The fact that capitalism first achieved a real and lasting breakthrough in Europe is, however, a structural event that demands explanation on several levels. The fragmentation and rivalries of feudal power structures gave more leeway to would-be capitalists than was ever permitted by the large agrarian empires, no matter how advanced their technical achievements. At the same time fertile soil, regular rainfall, a network of navigable rivers all contributed to productivity, market expansion and surplus generation once direct producers could avail themselves of heavy ploughs, animal power, windmills and watermills. Like others, Harman gives importance to the weakening of lordly power consequent upon peasant revolt and great plagues, but he also stresses the role of the printing press, the clock, new blast furnaces and new forms of animal husbandry. He believes that by the 14th century a mixed species of 'market feudalism' had developed, and that the social and military strife launched by the Reformation was greatly to weaken the feudal element and to promote a new social landscape more conducive to the rise of independent producers and merchants.

Perhaps the reason for Harman's peremptory treatment of prior debates on the transition stems from the fact that they have focused on structure, not narrative. Consequently they cannot readily be used to interpret the striking sequence of bourgeois revolution and capitalist advance in such events as the Reformation, the Peasant War in Germany, the religious wars in France, the revolt of the Netherlands, the Thirty Years War, the English Revolution, the Enlightenment, the war for American independence and the French Revolution. One of the most original features of this book is that it argues that each of these episodes ultimately strengthened the autonomy of capitalism, notwithstanding the great variety of the social forces which participated in these events and contrived to set their own stamp upon them. Indeed Harman evidently warms to the popular and heroic dimension of struggles against the old order and usually has less to say about the phase of bourgeois exploitation and consolidation. In the case of the English Revolution he evokes the revolutionary spirit of the Levellers and New Model Army, drawing on the work of Brian Manning and Ian Gentles, but has little to say about the Glorious Revolution of 1688-1689, which put such vital finishing touches on the new bourgeois order as the Bank of England and the National Debt. As John Brewer has shown in *The Sinews of Power*, it was these financial mechanisms which enabled the new regime to defeat its enemies at home and abroad. In his account of the American Revolution, Harman also dwells on its popular contribution with somewhat less attention paid to the advances of capitalism to which Gordon Wood has drawn attention.

This is a matter of emphasis only and one cannot complain that Harman neglects the bloodshed and oppression associated with capitalist accumulation. In my view Harman rightly stresses the contribution of colonial conquest and super-exploitation to the accumulation process while insisting that it was capitalism that gave rise to slavery and not slavery to capitalism. Some accounts of the capitalist rationality and the advantages of free wage labour fail to register that capitalism's reach was always greater than its grasp. Accumulation in the metropolis needed ongoing systems of primitive accumulation in the colonies because it had not yet managed completely to penetrate and transform the periphery. This is one of the reasons that a new breed of Atlantic merchants and planters were to play a leading role in the first wave of bourgeois revolutions. The slave systems they thus consolidated made necessary a second wave of struggles in which the new order was forced to jettison the most extreme forms of personal bondage, as Harman relates of the American Civil War.

In the dialectic of popular struggle and capitalist consolidation at least two possibilities are usually present, namely 'two steps forward, one step back' and 'one step forward, two steps back'. In other words there are no guarantees of social progress even where productive possibilities are expanding. The Nazi economic order managed to mobilise capitalist interests for a time more effectively than did the bourgeois democratic administrations in Washington, Paris and London. If Hitler had been content with his winnings in May 1941 the Nazi regime might have ruled Europe for a generation or more.

Harman's focus on politics and popular struggle helps to convey the drama which always attends the clash of rival social forces and regimes. This is especially true of his deft handling of the great sweep of world history from the 14th century down to the First World War. By the time we reach the middle and end of the 20th century Harman's story will be more familiar to most readers and his thumbnail sketch accounts less forceful. Harman briefly problematises capitalist democracy or the nature of the Second World War, but does not have the space to develop a rounded argument. On the latter, for example, it is not clear whether he thinks that the points he advances against Hobsbawm's claim that the war was fundamentally anti-fascist in nature add up to a flat contradiction or to an important qualification.

The account given by Harman of the rise of Nazism does not, in my view, sufficiently register the disastrous failure of the Social Democrats and Communists to form a democratic front. In my view Trotsky's grasp of the terrible threat in Germany was sounder than his sense of what was happening in France; on the evidence here Harman might put it the other way round. Likewise the boost given to social reform and decolonisation by the defeat of the Axis powers is somewhat underplayed. The narrative approach naturally tends to stress what happens rather than to note what does not happen. Thus Harman does not ponder the fact that workers' councils and soviet-type bodies did not arise in France in May 1968, or Portugal and Spain in the mid-1970s or in Eastern Europe and the Soviet Union in 1989. In all these cases the popular longing for a more democratic order was to be cheated to a greater or lesser extent but calls for 'workers' self management' or 'workers' power' seemed abstract if counterposed to elections based on universal suffrage.

But my reservations on such points detract little from my appreciation of Harman's achievement in this book. The dovetailed accounts of historical developments across seven or eight millennia are always interesting, usually well informed and sometimes highly original. The left has no dearth of polemics concerning the major events of the 20th century. On the other hand it has few accounts which convey as well as this book does the broad sweep of human history.

Notes

1   Those interested in such claims might like to consult A Maddison, *China's Growth in the Long Run* (New York, 1999).

In defence of Marxism

A review of Georg Lukács, A Defence of 'History and Class Consciousness': Tailism and the Dialectic (Verso, 2000), £16

JIM WOLFREYS

Although his work on the novel became hugely influential, the towering achievement of Georg Lukács' life remains *History and Class Consciousness*. But despite the book's status as a Marxist classic, there has always been a mystery at the heart of the debate sparked by its attack on determinism.

It was to be expected that those who held to a Second International emphasis on history's 'objective laws' of development, like Kautsky and leading members of the German KPD, would attack it. Neither was it surprising that prominent figures in the Soviet and Hungarian Communist parties, along with Soviet philosophers like Abram Deborin, should join in at a time when Marxism in Russia was becoming increasingly influenced by this kind of fatalism. What is curious, however, is that Lukács did not respond to the criticism. As Michael Löwy puts it, 'For ten years Lukács kept silent in the face of this philosophical barrage; it was an enigmatic silence which requires explanation, although we ourselves do not know of an adequate one'.[1] This book provides it and represents a sustained and vigorous defence of *History and Class Consciousness*.

Following its publication in 1923, *History and Class Consciousness* was subjected to ferocious criticism. Lukács publicly distanced himself from it on numerous occasions, first of all in 1933, later going as far as to unsuccessfully oppose its republication in a French edition in 1960, and then writing a preface to the 1967 English edition which denounced it as a book 'based on mistaken assumptions',[2] and tarnished by idealism, confusion and 'messianic utopianism'.[3]

In disowning *History and Class Consciousness* Lukács effectively turned his back on the classical Marxist tradition, a tradition which the book had powerfully reasserted and updated. As the 1920s wore on, he rallied to Stalin, and in 1929 his career as a leading member of the Hungarian Communist Party was curtailed when he was denounced at the party's second congress and forced to withdraw from active politics. Aside from a brief period during the 1956 Hungarian Revolution when Lukács took part in the anti-USSR Nagy government, and in the aftermath of the events of 1968 when he publicly voiced his opposition to the regimes of the Eastern bloc, Lukács devoted the last 40 years of his life to writing literary criticism and building a career as an academic philosopher.

History and Class Consciousness

For a brief period, then, Lukács played a significant role as an active revolutionary at the heart of the international communist movement at a time when socialism, in the wake of the Russian, German and Hungarian revolutions, was a genuine and immediate prospect for millions. This is the context in which *History and Class Consciousness* was written.

Central to the book is Marx's analysis of commodity production whereby relations between men take on the appearance of relations between things. Just as in religion, which creates the illusion that 'productions of the human brain appear as independent beings endowed with life, and entering into relation both with one another and the human race', so with the development of the market, 'the products of men's hands', commodities, appear to take on a life of their own. This Marx called the 'fetishism which attaches itself to the products of labour'.[4] Its effect was to obscure the fact that society and its institutions 'are just as much the products of men as linen, flax, etc'.[5] 'The objects of history', argued Lukács, 'appear as the objects of immutable, eternal laws of nature'.[6] Man therefore seemed powerless to influence the world around him.

Under capitalism, then, man is confronted with a reality which he has 'made', but which appears to be a natural phenomenon both alien to him and, moreover, in control of him. Lukács set out to demonstrate that this process of 'reification' applies not just to economic life but to the workings of society in its entirety. All of human life under capitalism is affected, from the institutions of the state to all intellectual and cultural activity. Ideas, opinions, even subjectivity are turned into commodities. Lukács famously described the journalist's 'lack of convictions' as the epitome of reification, whereby 'subjectivity itself, knowledge, temperament and powers of expression' are divorced from the personality of their owner and transformed into an autonomous and abstract mechanism.[7] In the same vein he cites Weber's description of judges as 'automatic statute-dispensing machines',[8] and Kant's characterisation of marriage as 'the union of two people of different sexes with a view to the mutual possession of each other's sexual attributes for the duration of their lives'.[9] The tendency towards greater and greater specialisation of skills under capitalism 'leads to the destruction of every image of the whole'.[10] In the case of modern science, the more developed it becomes, the more it turns into a 'formally closed system of partial laws', with the result that 'the world lying beyond its confines, and in particular the material base which it is its task to understand, *its own concrete underlying reality* lies, methodologically and in principle, *beyond its grasp*'.[11]

This analysis had important ramifications when it came to explaining how consciousness developed under capitalism. While the ruling class had at its disposal a whole array of ideological weapons (church, school, press, etc), the identification of workers with ruling class ideas (nationalism, racism, etc) could not be put down solely to indoctrination, important though this was. As society develops, the sense of powerlessness induced by reification not only 'sinks more deeply...into the consciousness of man',[12] but this feeling is experienced as something that seems normal and right, with the effect that feelings of deference and submission are generated spontaneously by workers as a consequence of their everyday experience of life under capitalism.

But this was not the whole story. Workers' position as the most exploited class gives rise to conflict over the form and duration of their exploitation. Their position in society therefore pushes workers into taking action against the injustice they suffer. In the process, they begin to understand their relationship to society in its totality. As a result of their own life experience workers discover within themselves the potential to change the course of history. History itself:

> ...*is no longer an enigmatic flux to which men and things are subjected. It is no longer a thing to be explained by the intervention of transcendental powers or made meaningful by reference to transcendental values. History is, on the one hand, the product (albeit the unconscious one) of man's own activity; on the other hand, it is the succession of those processes in which the forms taken by this activity and the relations of man to himself (to nature, to other men) are overthrown.*[13]

This puts the working class in a unique position as the only class capable of achieving true class consciousness ('the sense, become conscious, of the historical role of the class')[14] and of liberating humanity, since its own liberation can only be achieved through the abolition of class society. The bourgeoisie is incapable of achieving this consciousness, regardless of its insights into the laws of historical and economic development, since its role within the totality of society is to shore up its own minority rule against the interests of the majority: 'the barrier which converts the class consciousness of the bourgeoisie into "false" consciousness is objective; it is the class situation itself'.[15]

But although workers possess the capacity to understand society as a totality and their role within it, their immediate circumstances prevent them from grasping this. Hence Lukács insists on the distinction between 'false consciousness', or the day to day psychological or mass psychological consciousness of workers, and 'imputed consciousness', the consciousness which is objectively theirs. He illustrates this idea with a quote from Marx:

> The question is not what goal is **envisaged** for the time being by this or that member of the proletariat, or even by the proletariat as a whole. The question is **what is the proletariat** and what course of action will it be forced historically to take in conformity with its own **nature**.[16]

For Lukács' this concept of imputed consciousness is bound up with the Leninist model of the revolutionary party, since there is nothing inevitable about the process by which workers shake off their false consciousness and grasp their historic role. Revolution involves not only a struggle by the working class against an external enemy; it also requires an internal struggle against itself, 'against the devastating and degrading effects of the capitalist system upon its class consciousness'.[17] It is here that the revolutionary party plays a role in bridging the gap between 'false consciousness' and 'imputed consciousness', organising the most class conscious elements and striving to overcome the divisions and unevenness in workers' heads.

Criticism of *History and Class Consciousness*

By applying Marx's theory of alienation to the way in which consciousness develops under capitalism, Lukács brilliantly reaffirmed the Marxist method in the face of a growing tendency to transform historical materialism into an 'objective law' of historical development. In 1924, the year of Lenin's death, Lukács' work was subjected to a barrage of criticism. His comrade in the Hungarian Communist Party, Laszlo Rudas, attacked the notion of imputed consciousness as idealism. Lukács had presented the dialectic not as 'an objective theory of the laws of development of society and nature that is independent of man, but a theory of the subjective laws of man'.[18] Rudas was followed by Bukharin and then Zinoviev, general secretary of the Comintern, who condemned *History and Class Consciousness* as a work of 'theoretical revisionism'.[19]

In 1926, the year the Left Opposition was expelled from the Politburo as Stalin began to consolidate his leadership, Lukács published *Moses Hess and the Problems of Idealist Dialectics* in which he praised Hegel's reconciliation with the Prussian state as proof of his 'dialectical realism'.[20] In his study of Lukács, Michael Löwy shows how Hegel's accommodation to Thermidor, the post-revolutionary period of bourgeois rule, became, in Lukács' mind, a metaphor for his own reconciliation with Stalinism. In contrast to the poet Hölderlin, who remains a revolutionary and is 'broken by a reality which has no place for his ideals', Hegel 'builds up his philosophy precisely on an understanding of this new turning point in world history' and takes his place 'in the main current of the ideological development of his class'.[21]

The analogy between the respective paths taken by Lukács, who compromises with the Stalinist Thermidor in order, he hopes, to play an important role in an 'unheroic' but nevertheless 'progressive' period, and Trotsky, who refuses to compromise and is murdered, is clear. The former's denials and self criticisms thus become an 'entry ticket' to meaningful activity.[22] Lukács survived until 1971 but his compromise with Stalinism led him, as Marshall Berman puts it, 'to enlist actively in the fight against his life and thought',[23] poisoning and distorting his creativity and making of him 'one of the real tragic heroes of the 20th century'.[24]

History and Class Consciousness is in many ways a demanding work, not simply because of the level of theoretical abstraction, but because the book, a collection of essays written between 1919 and 1922 (the earliest of which were subsequently revised prior to publication), contained a number of ambiguities. Many of these, not least his apparent rejection of the notion of the dialectic in nature, were thrown back at Lukács by hostile critics. But a further problem for anyone wishing to understand *History and Class Consciousness* is that the book also has to be defended 'from its own author'.[25] The criticisms made by Lukács about the book's 'overriding subjectivism' in his extraordinary preface to the 1967 English edition were used to bolster a new round of attacks made by a number of prominent Althusserians. Criticism of Lukács centred on the question of the dialectic in nature and the question of imputed class consciousness. Lukács, it was argued, overestimated the role of the latter to such an extent that the attainment of class consciousness became a substitute for the 'brute, material struggle for power'.[26]

The most coherent of these criticisms, by Gareth Stedman Jones, used a selective reading of *History and Class Consciousness*[27] to accuse Lukács of idealism, claiming that he offered no epistemological basis for his concept of the revolutionary party whose role in transforming society is, according to Stedman Jones, at first reduced to insignificance by Lukács' insistence on the centrality of the miracle-working 'powers of consciousness',[28] and then, as Lukács flips from economic spontaneism to organisational voluntarism, invested with a 'mythical belief' in its, rather than workers' 'ideological efficacy'.[29] In any case, he argues, Lukács had no grasp of the complexities between party and class, and failed to show how the party compensates for the lag between working class consciousness and the objective crisis of society. Lukács fails to take into account either the institutional means by which ruling class ideology bolsters its power or the means by which workers' ideas may become contaminated by bourgeois ideology. Ultimately, Lukács does not see the working class as a concrete historical force but sees it in abstract and ethereal terms, as 'a hitherto missing term in a geometrical proof'.[30]

Forming the 'theoretical core' of *History and Class Consciousness* was Lukács' attack on science and technology. In rejecting positivism Lukács was guilty of scorning the natural sciences as examples of bourgeois false consciousness and ignoring the fact that 'the epistemology of a science is irreducible to its historical conditions of production'.[31] In the process, then, Lukács not only rejected Marx's emphasis on the progressive effects of industrialisation and technological advance, most importantly as a precondition for socialism, but also denied the possibility that historical materialism could be considered an autonomous science.

These criticisms were echoed elsewhere. Poulantzas referred to the inadequate theoretical status Lukács granted to ideologies, which were seen as simply the 'products' of consciousness or of freedom, alienated from the subject,[32] like 'numbers plates carried on the backs of class subjects'.[33] Leszek Kolakowski argued that Lukács 'endows Marxism with an irrational and anti-scientific character' which revealed 'the mythological, prophetic and utopian sense of Marxism'.[34]

Lukács was therefore variously presented as an idealist, a voluntarist and a theoretical apologist for Stalinism. Behind the seductive language and the references to Marx, Weber, Simmel and Kant critics spied a trickster philosopher who had taken the dialectic and replaced Hegel's metaphysical belief in the transcendent power of the 'Spirit' with an equally metaphysical belief in the power of the working class to acquire knowledge of class society and thereby put an end to it.

Tailism and the dialectic

Lukács' defence of *History and Class Consciousness*, presented here with an introduction by John Rees and a postface by Slavoj Žižek, is divided into two parts: the first dealing with the notion of imputed consciousness and the role of the revolutionary party in raising and generalising class consciousness, the second with the dialectic in nature. The defence begins with a statement of the aims of *History and Class Consciousness*:

> To demonstrate methodologically that the organisation and tactics of Bolshevism are the only possible consequence of Marxism; to prove that, of necessity, the problems of Bolshevism follow logically—that is to say logically in a dialectical sense—from the method of materialist dialectics as implemented by its founders.[35]

History and Class Consciousness, Lukács argues, was concerned with demonstrating the dialectical interaction between subject and object. To view consciousness simply as a reflection of the individual's position in the production process is to make subjective activity separate from, and dependent on, objective circumstances. Human activity is in this way subordinated to 'formal, transhistorical laws'.[36] Marxism is reduced to nothing more than bourgeois sociology. Politically, this results in 'tail-ending' or 'tailism': an accommodation to the general, rather than most advanced level of class consciousness on the basis that this consciousness will only be raised by changes in objective circumstances.

This interaction between subject and object or, to be more specific, the unique role of the working class as the only force able consciously to make its own history, can only be understood in relation to practical politics. Separated from concrete circumstances this interplay breaks down and becomes just another abstract concept, resulting in an idealist 'mythology of concepts'. The historical process will occasionally throw up 'moments' (here Lukács contrasts the October days in 1917 to the failed Hungarian Revolution) in which the essential tendencies of the process come to a head and demand action. The course of action taken will, in turn, determine the future development of the process. Objective circumstances can therefore be seen to be constituted in part by subjective action.

Failure to grasp the fact that the historical moment and the historical process form a differentiated unity, that they are distinct but not separate entities, means that the role of conscious, human intervention, in this case the role of the revolutionary party, is either underestimated (spontaneism) or exaggerated and turned into an 'empty phraseology of subjectivism' (ultra-leftism).[37] The key to understanding the historical process is therefore its contradictory nature, 'jerkily unfolding in advances and retreats in every—apparently—calm moment'.[38]

The thesis put forward at the Third Congress of the Comintern, that 'there is no moment when a Communist Party cannot be active', rings true, argues Lukács, since 'there can be no moment where this character of the process, the germ, the possibility of an active influencing of the subjective moments, is completely lacking'.[39] Revolutionary activity consists not in anticipating a time when the proletariat will reach ideological maturity, or of limiting its ideological influence to educational work, but in responding to 'the more concealed moments' neither with fatalism nor opportunism, but active intervention 'in the process of developing of proletarian class consciousness from its actual position to the highest level that is objectively possible'.[40] The centrality of Lukács' conception of the role of the party is clear:

> The proletariat can have a correct knowledge of the historical process and its individual stages on its causes and—most importantly—on the means of overcoming it, in accordance with its class position. But does it always have that knowledge? Not at all. And in as much as this distance is acknowledged to be a fact, it is the duty of every Marxist to seriously reflect.[41]

Does this mean Lukács overestimates the ideological aspects of the subjective factor at the expense of the 'brute, material struggle for power?' Crises, he argues, will throw up revolutionary situations but their resolution depends ultimately on the active and conscious intervention of the most class conscious vanguard. The art of insurrection, then, is 'one moment of the revolutionary process where the subjective moment has a decisive predominance'.[42]

In developing the guidelines for action and the slogans that flow from them the party is not engaged in simply handing down 'correct' consciousness from on high. The relationship between workers and a party attempting to raise and generalise the level of class consciousness must:

> ...be conceived as a relationship between permanently moving moments, as a process... This means that economic being, and, with it, proletarian class consciousness and its organisational forms, find themselves transformed uninterruptedly...that is why determinations such as level of class consciousness, the sense of historical role are not abstract and formal, not concepts that are fixed for all time, but express concrete relationships in concrete historical situations... This development, this raising of the level of class consciousness is, then, not an endless (or finite) progress, not a permanent advance towards a goal fixed for all time, but itself a dialectical process.[43]

The party's role is one of mediation. It acts as a link between the outward appearance of reality and its underlying essence. It arises out of both class struggle and consciousness and stands in a dialectical relationship to the class as an organisational form 'in which and through which develops and is developed the consciousness that corresponds to the social being of the proletariat'.[44]

The dialectic in nature

In the second half of his essay Lukács addresses the question of the dialectic in nature. The focus of this discussion, however, is not the issue which raised so much controversy in *History and Class Consciousness*, as to whether the dialectic in nature can be said to exist (Lukács does not dispute this point) but rather the way in which knowledge of nature is formed, and the role that knowledge plays in our relationship to nature.

The core of the controversy with Rudas is summed up as follows: 'Do people stand in an immediate relationship to nature, or is their metabolic interchange with nature mediated socially?'[45] In other words, as Žižek puts it in his provocative postface to the book, it 'is not sufficient to oppose the way things "objectively are" to the way they "merely appear to us": the way they appear (to the observer) affects their very "objective being".'[46] Moreover:

> ...when Lukács opposes the act of self consciousness of a historical subject to the 'correct insight' of natural sciences, his point is not to establish an epistemological distinction between two different methodological procedures, but, precisely, to break up the very standpoint of formal 'methodology' and to assert that **knowledge itself is part of social reality.**[47]

On the one hand, then, it is self evident that 'society arose from nature', that its laws existed before society and that the dialectic 'could not possibly be effective as an objective principle of development of society, if it were not already effective as a principle of development of nature before society, if it did not already objectively exist'.[48] But the dialectical conception of knowledge as a historical process implies both the discovery of previously unknown contents and objects, and the development of new principles of knowledge with which they can be understood. It also implies that the process of knowledge forms part of, and is therefore determined by, the particular stage of the objective social process of development.

Our relationship to nature is therefore subject to a 'double determination': firstly, as an interaction with nature (which exists independently of humans) and secondly, and simultaneously, the economic structure of society at any time. To claim, therefore, that the natural sciences exist independently of social being would imply that the natural scientist stands outside society. Lukács argues that various scientific categories which appear 'eternal' (taken directly from nature) may be seen to be historical. He cites Kautsky's observation that the replacement of theories of catastrophe in the natural sciences by theories of imperceptible development reflected the bourgeoisie's development from a revolutionary to a conservative class; and Marx's view that the conceptions of both Descartes, with regard to animals, and Lamettrie, with regard to humans, were shaped by 'the period of manufacture'.[49] Likewise, argued Marx, Darwin recognised 'in animals and plants his English society with its division of labour, competition, search for new markets, "inventions" and Malthus's "fight for existence".'[50]

Human knowledge, then, 'is determined according to its source'.[51] This is not a relativist argument for counterposing both primitive conceptions and modern natural science (both products of their time) to 'objective truth'. Instead Lukács argues that the level of knowledge achieved at any point in history is only relative in that its flaws can be exposed 'through a higher development of the economic structure of society'. But this is not to deny that this knowledge may be considered 'absolute truth', given that there is no external measure of objective truth standing outside society, and to the extent that this knowledge 'pertains to the objective reality of social being and the nature mediated through this'. The status of knowledge only changes once a more correct and comprehensive form of knowledge 'overcomes' it.[52]

Since it is axiomatic, argues Lukács, for Marxists to understand Egyptian astronomy or Aristotelian physics as products of their time, why should modern natural sciences be any different? In an important sense, however, they are different because they develop with capitalism, and it is only under capitalism that the economic structure of society and the 'true driving forces of its history' can be discerned. Moreover, whereas early capitalism inherited from feudalism elements of technology, it was the development of industry that unified them, producing the 'material, economic and social preconditions for socialism', and creating a formidable technological inheritance which socialist society will work with and develop and eventually transform.[53] An 'adequate, objective and systematic knowledge of nature' then is not only made possible by capitalism, it is 'a necessity for it', since capitalism requires an unprecedented command over natural forces.

The superiority of historical materialism over previous scientific methods lies in its comprehension of reality as a historical process and of knowledge as a product of this process. Lukács' insistence that knowledge of nature is socially mediated, and therefore that knowledge of society and knowledge of nature do not develop independently of each other, forms the basis of his 'attack' on the dialectic in nature since to view the two as separate reduces the dialectic to 'a principal of knowledge, a type of higher logic. That is to say it becomes idealistic'.[54] 'Historical materialism is not compelled to absolutise either the knowledge itself, or the present historical reality which determines the form and content of knowledge'.[55]

We are brought back, then, to Lukács' original attack on the tendency to see the dialectic as a set of objective laws of development. The appearance of things is not something to be stripped away like a veil, revealing the law-bound course of history beneath. Those like Rudas, who observe the fatalistic unfolding of history and 'anticipate' revolutionary developments, do not just follow events—the dialectic is robbed of its revolutionary implications, and 'tail-ending turns into apologia':[56]

> *It is clear* [from Marx] *that this capitalist husk is merely a husk, that 'behind' this husk (better inside this husk) those objective social forces that brought about capitalism, and which will lead to its demise, are effective... For the existence of this husk is inseparably tied up with the most essential forms of existence of our present social being (machines with division of labour in factories, division of labour in factories with social division of labour etc). With historical materialism we can reach an outlook onto those times where the real forms of being are really abolished...but we can not pre-empt this development concretely in thought. The actual disappearance of the capitalist husk happens in the real process of history: that is to say, in order to allow the capitalist husk to disappear concretely and actually those real categories of social being (capitalist division of labour, separation of town and country, of physical and mental labour) must be revolutionised'.[57]*

Conclusion

Tailism and the Dialectic offers more than a defence of *History and Class Consciousness* against those who condemned it on publication. It also presents a convincing rebuttal of many of the attacks made on it since its publication in English in 1967. More importantly, it offers a powerful restatement of the political and organisational consequences of Marxist dialectics first elaborated in the final essay of *History and Class Consciousness*, 'Towards a Methodology of the Problem of Organisation', and later in Lukács' 1924 biography of Lenin. In this sense, as John Rees points out in his introduction to the book, it forms part of a trilogy, with *History and Class Consciousness* and *Lenin*, and represents Lukács' 'last great affirmation of the formidable theoretical unity that he forged in *History and Class Consciousness* between a fully effective account of ideology and Lenin's theory of the party'.[58]

In the wake of the events of spring 1968, the Russian invasion of Czechoslovakia and the French May, Lukács told an interviewer, 'I suppose that the whole experiment that began in 1917 has now failed, and has to be tried again at some other time and place'.[59] After a lifetime as one of the most prolific writers of his generation, which embraced both the optimism of the revolutionary period opened up by 1917 and the appalling distortions of the Stalinist bureaucracy to which he himself became prey, practically the last words Lukács wrote were, 'Both systems in crisis. Authentic Marxism the only solution'.[60] This volume represents, from beyond the grave, a return to the revolutionary optimism of the early Lukács and a valuable tool for those seeking to pick up the thread of authentic Marxism broken by Stalin in the early 1920s.

Notes

1   M Löwy, *Georg Lukács: From Romanticism to Bolshevism* (London, 1979), p169.
2   G Lukács, *History and Class Consciousness* (London, 1983), pxxxvii.
3   Ibid, pxxviii.
4   K Marx, *Capital*, vol 1 (London 1983), p77.
5   K Marx, *The Poverty of Philosophy*, cited in G Lukács, op cit, p48.
6   Ibid, p48.
7   Ibid, p100.
8   Cited ibid, p96.
9   Cited ibid, p100.
10   Ibid, p103.
11   Ibid, p104.
12   Ibid, p93.
13   Ibid, p185.
14   Ibid, p73.
15   Ibid, p54.
16   K Marx, *The Holy Family*, cited ibid, p46.
17   G Lukács, op cit, p80.
18   Cited in A Arato and P Breines, *The Young Lukács and the Origins of Western Marxism* (London, 1979), p178.
19   Cited ibid, p180.
20   Cited M Löwy, op cit, p194.
21   Cited ibid, p196.
22   Cited in G Lukács, op cit, pxxx. The comparison, as Lukács implies himself in the 1967 preface to *History and Class Consciousness*, also applies between him and Karl Korsch.
23   M Berman, *Adventures in Marxism* (London, 1999), p185.
24   Ibid, p204.
25   M Markovic, 'The Critical Thought of Georg Lukács', in T Rockmore (ed), *Lukács Today. Essays in Marxist Philosophy* (Dordrecht, 1988), p25.
26   G Stedman Jones, 'The Marxism of the Early Lukács', in *New Left Review* (ed) *Western Marxism: A Critical Reader* (London, 1977), p45.
27   For an excellent summary of Lukács' contribution to Marxism and a rebuttal of Stedman Jones's criticisms see J Rees, *The Algebra of Revolution: The Dialectic and the Classical Marxist Tradition* (London, 1998), pp202-261.
28   Stedman Jones, op cit, pp45-47.

29   Ibid, p43.
30   Ibid, p37.
31   Ibid, pp57-58.
32   N Poulantzas, *Political Power and Social Classes* (London, 1976), p196.
33   Ibid, p205.
34   Cited in M Hevesi, 'Lukács in the Eyes of Western Philosophy Today', in T Rock-more (ed), op cit, p48.
35   G Lukács, *A Defence of 'History and Class Consciousness': Tailism and the Dialectic* (London, 2000), p47.
36   Ibid, p50.
37   Ibid, p59.
38   Ibid, pp61-62.
39   Ibid, p62.
40   Ibid, pp67-68.
41   Ibid, p66.
42   Ibid, p22.
43   Ibid, pp77-78.
44   Ibid, pp78-79.
45   Ibid, p96.
46   S Žižek, 'Georg Lukács as the Philosopher of Leninism', in G Lukács, *A Defence of History and Class Consciousness*, op cit, p171.
47   Ibid, p171.
48   G Lukács, *A Defence of History and Class Consciousness*, op cit, p102.
49   Ibid, p131. This point is briefly made in *History and Class Consciousness*, pp130-131. Steven Rose makes the same point about the way scientists have perceived the workings of the brain, first on hydraulic principles, then as telephone exchanges, now as supercomputers. See S Rose, *Lifelines* (London,1997), p53.
50   G Lukács, *A Defence of History and Class Consciousness*, op cit, p104.
51   Ibid, p104.
52   Ibid, p105.
53   Ibid, p114.
54   Ibid, p108.
55   Ibid, pp105-106.
56   Ibid, p135.
57   Ibid, p134.
58   J Rees, introduction to ibid, p32.
59   Cited in M Berman, op cit, p204.
60   Ibid, p204.

Can capitalism be sustained?

A review of David Harvey, **The Limits to Capital** *(Verso, 1999), £18*

JUDY COX

Goodbye to all that

David Harvey is well known as the author of the influential *The Condition of Postmodernity* and before that as a champion of Marxist economics. The publication of a new edition of *The Limits to Capital* marks the revival of interest in Marxist accounts of capitalism. Even before 1998, when the crisis which had been developing in the South East Asian economies threatened to submerge the world economy under a tidal wave of bankruptcies and closures, a backlash against neo-liberal free market economics had begun. Neo-liberalism had dominated the 1980s, but 'Margaret Thatcher, Ronald Reagan and Newt Gingrich now appear as somewhat ghostly figures from some strange era when they held unchallenged power and influence', while critics of the system have multiplied in number. As early as 1996, the Davos Symposium (the global think-tank of neo-liberalism) worried that 'free market globalisation was a "brakeless train wreaking havoc" and that the "mounting backlash against its effects" was threatening to disrupt economic activity and social stability in many countries, promoting a mood of "helplessness and anxiety" in the industrial democracies that could all too easily "turn into revolt".'[1]

Harvey lists the growing number of influential writers and philosophers who are developing critiques of capitalism and, to differing degrees, rehabilitating Marx. His list includes Pierre Bourdieu, Richard

Rorty and Jacques Derrida. Even mainstream publications like *The New Yorker* could proclaim in 1997 that Karl Marx would be the 'next great thinker'. Harvey asks, 'With all this fluttering going on in the wings, can that other spectre—the communist alternative—be far behind?' His book is an attempt to provide this alternative. In it, he restates some of Marx's key ideas and defends them from various criticisms, but this is no mere 'exercise in nostalgia'. Harvey extends the framework Marx developed to include the ever-expanding financial sector and geographical aspects of capital accumulation. This book is a considerable achievement. His analysis has great historical breadth and theoretical depth. In this review I will try to give a flavour of Harvey's writing and look at some of the particular strengths and weaknesses of his analysis.

It must be borne in mind that this book is at times densely argued and technical but, as Marx pointed out, 'There is no royal road to science.' In *Capital* Marx approaches the economy as a series of interconnected relationships. This approach means that his explanations depend on the introduction of concepts which have not yet themselves been properly explained. Harvey points out how this dialectical method is very different from the bourgeois 'building block' approach or the 'linear' approach adopted by some Marxists, who search for a straight, well-signed path to economic enlightenment. Harvey follows Marx's lead and focuses on the intertwined relationships between the diverse elements of the economy. He also follows Marx's *Capital* by beginning with an analysis of the labour theory of value, then introducing ever more comprehensive accounts of the economy as a whole.

Commodities, values and prices

Harvey outlines Marx's insight that the basis of human society lies in the appropriation of nature through production and consumption. Under capitalism this takes place through the production and exchange of commodities, which have two aspects. They have a 'material side', the physical properties which enable them to satisfy human, social needs. Human beings produced objects with such use values before capitalism developed, but today use values should not be seen as ahistorical and independent of the economic relations dominating their production.

However, when we exchange commodities on the market we do not swap equivalent use values—rather we buy and sell for money. Thus, commodities have an exchange value as well as a use value. The prices we pay appear to be fixed naturally by the fluctuations of supply and demand. To look beneath this appearance Harvey turns to Marx's explanation of the origins and role of money. Although we take its existence for granted, money is not some natural product. It emerged out of the social process of commodity exchange which needed one commodity to be a 'universal equivalent', a socially accepted measure which could express the relative values of all the other commodities. Potentially, money could be either hoarded or thrown into circulation as a means of balancing the quantity of goods produced with the size of the market for them. However, through competition, capitalists are driven to constantly throw their capital into circulation, however damaging the results are for the system as a whole.

Harvey argues that the existence of money enabled Marx to draw his unique distinction between the two kinds of labour involved in the production of commodities. The specific labour embodied in every commodity he called concrete labour. In addition to the concrete labour which created it, each commodity represents a portion of the total labour being performed in society. This Marx called abstract labour. In the process of exchange only the amount of labour which is socially necessary to produce the commodity under average conditions, with average levels of skill, will be considered valuable. It is the quantity of socially necessary labour embodied in different commodities, rather than all the diverse types of concrete labour involved, which can be compared and thus provides the source of all commodity's exchange values. This understanding of how socially necessary labour time creates a benchmark which all capitalists must strive to equal and beat is central to Harvey's conception of the economy. It is an insight which he extends to other areas of the economy, as we shall see below.

Harvey, like Marx, understands capitalism as a process rather than a thing, a process which involves expanding value through a cycle of investment, production and exchange. Marx's unique contribution in analysing this process was to understand where profits come from, a factor which his contemporaries stumbled over. The labourer has no independent access to the means of production and therefore has to sell their ability to work for a specified period. However, the magnitude of value they produce is much greater than the value of the labour power the capitalist buys: the worker produces surplus value. Beneath the apparent freedom of individuals in a capitalist society exists compulsion— to produce at competitive speeds, to increase the rate of accumulation. This can be achieved in several ways, such as increasing absolute exploitation by lengthening the working week. Alternatively, capitalists can open up a gap between the socially necessary labour time operating in their industry and their own private costs of production by increasing 'the productivity of social labour, which becomes the most powerful lever of accumulation'.[2] This opens up the possibility for a conflict between the private interests and the class needs of the capitalist which can destabilise the whole system.

Harvey addresses general objections to Marx's theory by emphasising that value theory is not an accounting tool to be proved by calculations. He acknowledges other effective defences of the theory—by Rubin, Rosdolsky, and Fine and Harris—but he argues that even these sympathetic accounts fall short of capturing the true revolutionary significance of Marx's theory. Value theory is nothing less than a mechanism for understanding how the 'living life-giving fire' of labour becomes objectified into the fixed form of commodities and exchange rates by the iron discipline of capital.[3]

At every stage of his account of capitalism Harvey assesses the continuing relevance of the labour theory of value and answers detailed criticisms levelled against it. One such criticism relates to the way the growth of monopoly capitalism enables 'price fixing'. Marx explained how the law of value was modified when commodities were sold on the market. Competitive mechanisms tend to equalise prices and the rate of profit across different sectors of the economy, as investment flows into more profitable sectors, increasing production and so lowering the prices and profits generated there. Consequently, some have argued that the development of large monopolies that can 'fix prices' represents a movement away from the 'authority' of competition and therefore a movement away from the law of value. However, Harvey argues, capitalism was never a system of perfect competition, and competition takes many forms besides those that attach to price competition in the market. Rather, capitalism is constantly opening up new areas of competition, for example in state institutions, 'that permit the law of value to operate in diverse but ever more effective ways'.[4]

Another detailed criticism has been raised in relation to what happens during the process of production itself: fixed capital (machinery, factories, transport) transfers the value it embodies to the commodities it produces. Yet, critics have argued, the quantity of value in the fixed capital varies because improvements in production may make it quicker and easier to produce the same type of machines, thus decreasing the value of those already in operation. Thus, it is argued, the value of fixed capital transfers cannot simply relate to the labour value the fixed capital embodies. However, as Harvey points out, the concept of socially necessary labour time was always central to Marx's theory—he expected 'revolutions in value' to occur during production. So, Harvey concludes, 'Marx's comment that the law of value asserts itself like a "a law of nature" under capitalism was not a chance or flippant remark', and can be sustained.[5]

Production and exchange

Harvey moves from discussing the production of value to the realisation of that value through exchange. He criticises Say's Law, which stated that the supply of commodities automatically creates sufficient demand for them. While production and consumption are intertwined, as completing one involves creating the other, this does not necessarily create a match between sales and purchases. Rather, each act of buying and selling is part of a network of similar movements, each being an independent transaction, 'whose complementary transaction...does not need to follow immediately but may be separated from it temporarily and spatially'.[6] Capitalists seeking to sell their goods must do more than fulfil a social need—they must find effective need, need backed up by the ability to pay. However, production is driven to the limit of the productive forces without regard to the size of the market. This creates the potential for a crisis of overproduction. The 'merry-go-round of perpetual accumulation is not an automated or even a well-oiled machine'.[7]

Capitalism has a 'turnover' time, which is the time taken both to produce the commodity and to realise its value through exchange, but again this is not necessarily a smooth process. If capital is halted at any stage of its circulation, if goods go unsold or money lies idle, capital is frozen and becomes devalued.[8] As Marx pointed out, the optimum for capitalism is to move from production to exchange, from commodity to money, 'at the speed of thought'. Therefore, Harvey argues that just as there is a socially necessary labour time which provides the basis of commodity's value, so there is a 'socially necessary turnover time' which capitalists must strive to match. This means that their drive to reduce the time and costs of circulation of capital is a crucial part of their drive to accumulate.

Over-accumulation and crises

'We have, Marx asserts, built a vast social enterprise which dominates us, delimits our freedoms and ultimately visits upon us the worst forms of degradation. The irrationality of such a system becomes most evident at times of crisis'.[9] The potential conflicts and unevenness between different aspects of production and exchange which threaten crises, and the impossibility of regulation are constant themes of Harvey's book. In formulating his analysis of economic crises, Harvey builds a model based on three different levels of analysis.

First cut theory of the crisis: To accumulate capital, the capitalist must invest in both raw materials, plant and machinery, fixed capital, and in employing a workforce, variable capital. The drive to increase the productivity of labour fuels an accelerating spiral of technological change which means that the ratio of fixed capital to variable capital varies across different units of capital. The productivity of labour, measured in terms of raw material used and goods produced, Marx called the technical composition of capital. The relationship between the technical composition of a unit of capital and the value embodied in it Marx called the organic composition of capital.[10] As individual capitalists seek to beat the socially necessary labour time for producing commodities in their sector, they invest in more and more technology and the organic composition of capital rises. As labour, the source of surplus value, is squeezed out, the rate of profit for the whole capitalist class tends to fall.

Marx called this the most important law of political economy, yet Harvey does not accept its centrality. I will return to the implications of this below, but Harvey nevertheless explains how Marx's theory reveals other reasons for the recurrence of economic crises under capitalism. For example, he suggests that the constant revolutionising of the methods of production means that balanced accumulation becomes impossible. Marx's investigations of the falling rate of profit reveal a fundamental contradiction between the forces of production and the social relations of production. This contradiction arises as individual capitalists seek to improve their position relative to others in a way which is detrimental to the overall 'technological mix' necessary for the balanced accumulation of capital. Harvey argues that the concept of the organic composition of capital combined with the labour theory of value express this contradiction.

In addition, the falling rate of profit convincingly demonstrates that accumulation creates a surplus of capital relative to opportunities to employ that capital, the over-accumulation of capital. This can be mitigated for the system as a whole through the devaluation of capital which can occur when, for example, technological change involves the premature, involuntary retirement of the now obsolete machinery. Devaluation may counter over-accumulation in the system, but it is dangerous for the individual capitalist, who is driven to finish the cycles of production more and more quickly to avoid the risk. Thus, machinery or fixed capital, 'one of the chief means employed to increase the productivity of social labour, becomes, once it is installed, a barrier to further innovation'.[11] Devaluation can also be the result of high inflation, 'the social form of devaluation in modern times',[12] but it cannot provide a smooth, painless antidote to over-accumulation. Crises, which Harvey calls the irrational rationaliser of the economic system, can effectively devalue chunks of capital through bankruptcy and takeovers. Crises can prepare the way for a new round of accumulation but they are very dangerous for the individual capitalist.

Second cut theory of crisis: The crisis rooted in the arena of production must be integrated with the crisis which occurs in the financial system.

Today, the organised power of the financial system is 'mysterious because of sheer complexity' and its independence from democratic control. Harvey suggests that finance capital can be understood as the movement of all capital involved in providing credit, 'a contradiction-laden flow of interest-bearing capital'.[13] Such money capital can take many different forms—coins, paper currencies, credit monies—which can best be interpreted as 'an outcome of the drive to perfect money as a frictionless, costless and instantaneously adjustable "lubricant" of exchange while preserving the quality of the money as a measure of value'.[14]

The credit system unites those with capital and no outlet for investment with those who have a plan for production but lack the wherewithal to implement it. Harvey invokes the image of a 'central nervous system' which can co-ordinate the activities of individual capitalists. The credit system appears to have the potential to overcome imbalances between production and consumption, and production and realisation, but there are restrictions to this happening in practice. So, for example, powerful independent financiers are also subject to the laws of competition and the credit system can itself become a site of intense factional struggles. Furthermore, the credit system creates the possibility of insane bouts of speculation on interest rates and future profits. The fictitious values exchanged on the stock market increasingly diverge from the real values existing in the economy. Thus, while credit helped accelerate the material development of the productive forces and world market, it also accelerates the onset of crises. The financial sector remains incapable of dealing with fundamental questions of over-accumulation.

The 'second cut' theory of crisis integrates contradictions in financial and monetary aspects of the system with production, and distinguishes between temporary cyclical crises and long term decline resulting from internal contradictions. Furthermore, as crises embrace legal institutional and political frameworks of capitalist society, their resolution depends increasingly on deployment of naked military power.

Third cut theory of crisis: The accumulation of capital takes place during particular time scales in specific geographical locations. In order to explore the implications of this, Harvey embarks upon a theoretical discussion of the concept of rent which indicates the importance of spatial organisation to capital accumulation. Just as faster than average production times can create excess profits, so more favoured locations, those closer to raw materials or markets, can attract excess profits. Geographical locations are altered by human agency, by the building of new urban areas and transport systems, for example. The stimulus to build new environments and to revolutionise transport relations arises out of the need to shorten the circulation time of commodities and accelerate the turnover time of capital.

Harvey argues that spatial organisation is not just a reflection of accumulation processes, but rather is fundamental to the 'linking of commodity production in different locations through exchange'. The socially necessary transport costs form part of the value of the commodity, but this depends not on physical distance, but the speed with which distance can be travelled. Marx wrote how capital must 'strive to tear down every spatial barrier to...exchange, and conquer the whole earth for its market' and 'annihilate this space with time, to turn over capital in the "twinkling of an eye".'[15]

There are, however, barriers to speeding up the turnover time. Changing the location of production to a more favourable site requires the mobility of labour. Yet workers are subject to contradictory pressures in relation to immigration, and legal restrictions can stop labour moving to meet capital's needs. Similar contradictory requirements apply to the movement of money capital. Credit monies roam the world as fast as information can move, but they too encounter social barriers posed by the existence of different currencies of varying quality. It can be necessary to place restrictions on the movement of money to protect currencies and maintain the quality of the money.

Moreover, capitalism's chase of favoured locations carries its own inherent contradictions. In creating 'built environments', places with the material resources necessary for accumulation, larger amounts of capital are embedded in particular landscapes and areas. The fear of this fixed capital becoming devalued can become a barrier to revolutionising technology. Thus 'both capital and labour can become more geographically mobile at the price of freezing a portion of the total social capital in one place'.[16] Harvey argues that financial arrangements, the advancing of credit, can shape built environments according to the requirements of capital, but at the cost of the growth of property markets which exacerbate bouts of insane speculation. However, here as elsewhere, crisis can restore the health of the system: 'Rampant speculation and unchecked appropriation, costly as these are for capital and life-sapping as they may be for labour, generate the chaotic ferment out of which new spatial configurations can grow'.[17]

Some debates

The falling rate of profit: There is much that is fascinating and useful about Harvey's account of capital, the contradictory role of money and credit, the imbalances between production and consumption, the impact of the devaluation of fixed capital, and much more that is beyond the scope of this review. However, like some other Marxists, Harvey dismisses the tendency of the rate of profit to fall too abruptly. After all, Marx argued that just as the search for profits was central to capitalism, so a fall in the rate of profit threatened the whole basis of production.

Harvey suggests that Marx was too strongly influenced by his fellow political economists in his acceptance of the tendency of the rate of profit to fall. He levels other criticisms against the theory and the 'motley array' of countervailing factors which Marx argued could temporarily prevent the rate of profit falling. Perhaps his most important objection is his argument that the falling rate of profit cannot be treated as a historical or empirical proposition: 'We cannot, for example, assemble data on corporate profits in the United States since 1945 and prove or disprove the law by appeal to that particular historical record'.[18] This is mistaken on two counts, empirically and theoretically. Firstly, it *is* possible to examine the rate of profit, and those that have have found that, while the organic composition of capital has not risen continually since Marx's day, it has once again begun to rise.[19] Secondly, Marx did not suggest that the rate of profit would fall inexorably until capitalism collapsed. On the contrary, he argued that competition generated a constant downward pressure on the rate of profit which could be eased by countervailing tendencies, sometimes for prolonged periods. These countervailing tendencies were a central element of Marx's theory. He argued that they were built into the structure of capitalism, rather than being the superficial, secondary factors which appear in Harvey's account. Some countervailing tendencies, such as increasing the rate of exploitation, rationalising the system through bankruptcy and spending on arms, which do not feed back into the organic composition of other sectors of the economy, are all operating in the world economy today, although with decreasing impact on maintaining the rate of profit. It is only with reference to the falling rate of profit that we can understand why economic crises tend to get deeper and more prolonged as the system ages. In addition, a decline in the rate of profit generates intensified competition among the capitalists, leading to instability and conflict. It is this theory which explains why the very holy grail the capitalists seek, the increasing productivity of labour, also sows the seed of their downfall, as it lowers the rate of profit for the capitalist class.

The revolutionary working class: 'The violent destruction of capital, not by relations external to it, but rather as a condition of its self preservation, is the most striking form in which advice is given for it to be gone and to give room to a higher state of social production,' wrote Marx.[20] But what force is capable of driving capitalism from the stage? Harvey writes with great feeling about the madness of the system, but he seems to be less confident that the working class can break free of capitalism. In fact, he asks whether increasing material living standards in advanced capitalist countries have actually increased workers' dependency on capitalism. He correctly notes that 'the undoubted revelatory power of Marxian theory does not by itself guarantee its absorption by the proletariat as a guide to action'.[21] However, he makes the theoretical possibility of such a transformation less likely by suggesting that Marx believed workers are doomed to fail in their struggles against the impact of exploitation.

To develop this theme Harvey interweaves Marx's account of the labour process with that put forward by Harry Braverman in *Labor and Monopoly Capital* (1973). The production process involves workers' subjection to capital through the division of labour and specialisation, which makes capital richer in production power by making the individual worker poorer. It is a process which involves hierarchical, despotic scientific management, Fordism and Taylorism, which, Braverman reveals, 'penetrate within the very psychological makeup of the workers themselves'.[22] Harvey discusses criticisms of Marx and Braverman which accuse them of treating workers as hopelessly alienated, uncritical absorbers of capitalist ideologies. Here, some further weaknesses in Harvey's analysis emerge. He suggests that Marx dismissed workers' daily experiences as 'false consciousness', and that Marxist theory has never adequately resolved the duality of the worker as an 'object for capital' and a 'living creative subject'.[23]

Harvey suggests that this weakness may be remedied by the integration of Marxism with psychological theories. Yet the resolution of these issues can be found in the dialectical possibilities of Marx's theory of alienation and Lukács's development of the concept of commodity fetishism. Workers are atomised and made to feel powerless by the organisation of capitalist society, their lack of control over the processes of production, and the way in which social relationships are experienced as relationships between physical objects outside the control of human beings. However, at the same time there exists a constant pressure for workers to organise collectively and struggle against capitalism, creating a constant tension between the experience of alienation and the experience of exercising real collective power. Even struggles for basic improvements, such as that to shorten the length of the working day, involve a potential challenge to the laws of the market in which the true, social nature of production can be laid bare. Lukács wrote how 'this is the point where the "eternal laws" of capitalist economics fail and become dialectical, and are thus compelled to yield up the decisions regarding the fate of history of the conscious actions of men'.[24] The tension between the alienated condition of workers and their potential power to remake society frequently erupts in class struggles, but it can only be finally resolved by the political and economic victory of the working class.

Conclusion

The fact that Harvey's book has been reprinted is itself testimony to the revival of interest in Marxist economics. Some of the ideas in this book were developed in *The Condition of Postmodernity*, which moved away from Marx's economic theories in favour of cultural change and exploring the 'time-space compression' of modern society. But *The Limits to Capital* is an important book, albeit one which is not, as may by now be obvious, designed for those who are new to Marxist economics. For those who want to develop their understanding of key Marxist concepts, to engage with original ideas about the spatial organisation of our world, and to confront challenges to and debates about Marx's theory of crisis, this book is recommended.

Notes

1   D Harvey, *The Limits to Capital* (Verso, 1999), pxvi.
2   Ibid, p159.
3   Harvey provides some very important comments on two of the great controversies that have arisen from Marx's analysis of value. The first relates to how wages are distributed among members of the working class who have varying degrees of skill, a process Harvey roots in the development of the wage labour system. He later suggests that skilled labour, which Marx reduced theoretically to a standard unit of unskilled labour, is today reduced in practice through the division of labour in the workplace. The second controversy focuses on how the tendency for the rate of profit to equalise across the economy transforms the labour values of commodities into prices of production when they are sold on the market. Harvey argues that these prices of production are still based on values rather than market prices. Capitalists tend to respond to these prices of production, rather than obscured real requirements for surplus value, which means they act in a way which can threaten the basis of their own social reproduction. Ibid, p68fn.
4   Ibid, p153.
5   Ibid, p141.
6   Quoted ibid, p85.
7   Ibid, p96.
8   Ibid, p85.
9   Ibid, p203.
10   Chris Harman gives the following definition of these concepts: 'Marx called the ratio of the physical extent of the means of production to the amount of labour power employed on them the "technical composition of capital", and the ratio of the value of the means of production to the value of the labour power employed the "organic composition".' C Harman, *Explaining the Crisis* (Bookmarks, 1984), p18.
11   D Harvey, op cit, p123.
12   Ibid, p197.
13   Ibid, p317.
14   Ibid, p251.

15   Ibid, p377.
16   Ibid, p398.
17   Ibid, p398.
18   Ibid, p181.
19   See J Geier and A Shawki, 'Contradictions of the "Miracle" Economy',
      International Socialist Review 2, Autumn 1997; C Harman, op cit, ch 3.
20   Quoted in D Harvey, op cit, p197.
21   Ibid, p113.
22   Ibid, p110.
23   Ibid, p114.
24   Quoted in J Rees, *The Algebra of Revolution* (Routledge, 1998), p222.

The Socialist Workers Party is one of an international grouping of socialist organisations:

AUSTRALIA   International Socialists, PO Box A338,
                   Sydney South
BRITAIN   Socialist Workers Party, PO Box 82, London E3
CANADA   International Socialists, PO Box 339, Station E,
                   Toronto, Ontario M6H 4E3
CYPRUS   Ergatiki Demokratia, PO Box 7280, Nicosia
DENMARK   Internationale Socialister, PO Box 5113, 8100
                   Aarhus C
GERMANY   Linksruck, Postfach 304 183, 20359 Hamburg
GREECE   Sosialistiko Ergatiko Komma, c/o Workers
                   Solidarity, PO Box 8161, Athens 100 10
HOLLAND   Internationale Socialisten, PO Box 92052, 1090AA
                   Amsterdam
IRELAND   Socialist Workers Party, PO Box 1648, Dublin 8
NEW ZEALAND   Socialist Workers Organization, PO Box 8851,
                   Auckland
NORWAY   Internasjonale Socialisterr, Postboks 9226
                   Grønland, 0134 Oslo
POLAND   Solidarność Socjalistyczna, PO Box 12,
                   01-900 Warszawa 118
SPAIN   Socialismo Internacional, Apartado 563, 08080
                   Barcelona
UNITED STATES International Socialist Organisation, PO Box
                   16085, Chicago, Illinois 60616
ZIMBABWE   International Socialist Organisation, PO Box 6758,
                   Harare

The following issues of *International Socialism* (second series) are available price £3 (including postage) from IS Journal, PO Box 82, London E3 3LH. *International Socialism* 2:58 and 2:65 are available on cassette from the Royal National Institute for the Blind (Peterborough Library Unit). Phone 01733 370777.

International Socialism 2:85 Winter 1999
Alex Callinicos: Reformism and class polarisation in Europe ★ Michael Lavalette and Gerry Mooney: New Labour, new moralism: the welfare politics and ideology of New Labour under Blair ★ Ken Coates: Benign imperialism versus United Nations ★ John Baxter: Is the UN an alternative to 'humanitarian imperialism'? ★ John Rose: Jesus: history's most famous missing person ★ Chris Harman: The 20th century: an age of extremes or an age of possibilities? ★ Mike Gonzalez: Is modernism dead? ★ Peter Morgan: The man behind the mask ★ Anne Alexander: All power to the imagination ★ Anna Chen: George Orwell: a literary Trotskyist? ★ Rob Hoveman: History of theory ★ Chris Harman: Comment on Molyneux on art

International Socialism 2:84 Autumn 1999
Neil Davidson: The trouble with 'ethnicity' ★ Jim Wolfreys: Class struggles in France ★ Phil Marfleet: Nationalism and internationalism ★ Tom Behan: The return of Italian Communism ★ Andy Durgan: Freedom fighters or Comintern army? The International Brigades in Spain ★ John Molyneux: Art, alienation and capitalism: a reply to Chris Nineham ★ Judy Cox: Dreams of equality: the levelling poor of the English Revolution

International Socialism 2:83 Summer 1999
John Rees: The socialist revolution and the democratic revolution ★ Mike Haynes: Theses on the Balkan War ★ Angus Calder: Into slavery: the rise of imperialism ★ Jim Wolfreys: The physiology of barbarism ★ John Newsinger: Scenes from the class war: Ken Loach and socialist cinema ★

International Socialism 2:82 Spring 1999
Lindsey German: The Blair project cracks ★ Dan Atkinson and Larry Elliott: Reflating Keynes: a different view of the crisis ★ Peter Morgan: The new Keynesians: staking a hold in the system? ★ Rob Hoveman: Brenner and crisis: a critique ★ Chris Nineham: Art and alienation: a reply to John Molyneux ★ Paul McGarr: Fascists brought to book ★ Brian Manning: Revisionism revised ★ Neil Davidson: In perspective: Tom Nairn ★

International Socialism 2:81 Winter 1998
Alex Callinicos: World capitalism at the abyss ★ Mike Haynes and Pete Glatter: The Russian catastrophe ★ Phil Marfleet: Globalisation and the Third World ★ Lindsey German: In a class of its own ★ Judy Cox: John Reed: reporting on the revolution ★ Kevin Ovenden: The resistible rise of Adolf Hitler ★

International Socialism 2:80 Autumn 1998
Clare Fermont: Indonesia: the inferno of revolution ★ Workers' representatives and socialists: Three interviews from Indonesia ★ Chris Bambery: Report from Indonesia ★ Tony Cliff: Revolution and counter-revolution: lessons for Indonesia ★ John Molyneux: The legitimacy of modern art ★ Gary McFarlane: A respectable trade? Slavery and the rise of capitalism ★ Paul McGarr: The French Revolution: Marxism versus capitalism ★ Shaun Doherty: Will the real James Connolly please stand up? ★

International Socialism 2:79 Summer 1998
John Rees: The return of Marx? ★ Lindsey German: Reflections on *The Communist Manifesto* ★ Judy Cox: An introduction to Marx's theory of alienation ★ Judith Orr: Making a comeback: the Marxist theory of crisis ★ Megan Trudell: New Labour, old conflicts: the story so far ★ John Molyneux: State of the art ★ Anna Chen: In perspective: Sergei Eisenstein ★ Jonathan Neale: Vietnam veterans ★ Phil Gasper: Bookwatch: Marxism and science ★

International Socialism 2:78 Spring 1998
Colin Sparks: The eye of the storm ★ Shin Gyoung-hee: The crisis and the workers' movement in South Korea ★ Rob Hoveman: Financial crises and the real economy ★ Peter Morgan: Class divisions in the gay community ★ Alex Callinicos: The secret of the dialectic ★ John Parrington: It's life, Jim, but not as we know it ★ Judy Cox: Robin Hood: earl, outlaw or rebel? ★ Ian Birchall: The vice-like hold of nationalism? A comment on Megan Trudell's 'Prelude to revolution' ★ William Keach: In perspective: Alexander Cockburn and Christopher Hitchens ★

International Socialism 2:76 Autumn 1997
Mike Haynes: Was there a parliamentary alternative in 1917? ★ Megan Trudell: Prelude to revolution: class consciousness and the First World War ★ Judy Cox: A light in the darkness ★ Pete Glatter: Victor Serge: writing for the future ★ Gill Hubbard: A guide to action ★ Chris Bambery: Review article: Labour's history of hope and despair ★

International Socialism 2:75 Summer 1997
John Rees: The class struggle under New Labour ★ Alex Callinicos: Europe: the mounting crisis ★ Lance Selfa: Mexico after the Zapatista uprising ★ William Keach: Rise like lions? Shelley and the revolutionary left ★ Judy Cox: What state are we really in? ★ John Parrington: In perspective: Valentin Voloshinov ★

International Socialism 2:74 Spring 1997
Colin Sparks: Tories, Labour and the crisis in education ★ Colin Wilson: The politics of information technology ★ Mike Gonzalez: No more heroes: Nicaragua 1996 ★ Christopher Hill: Tumults and commotions: turning the world upside down ★ Peter Morgan: Capitalism without frontiers? ★ Alex Callinicos: Minds, machines and evolution ★ Anthony Arnove: In perspective: Noam Chomsky★

International Socialism 2:73 Winter 1996
Chris Harman: Globalisation: a critique of a new orthodoxy ★ Chris Bambery: Marxism and sport ★ John Parrington: Computers and consciousness: a reply to Alex Callinicos ★ Joe Faith: Dennett, materialism and empiricism ★ Megan Trudell: Who made the American Revolution? ★ Mark O'Brien: The class conflicts which shaped British history ★ John Newsinger: From class war to Cold War ★ Alex Callinicos: The state in debate ★ Charlie Kimber: Review article: coming to terms with barbarism in Rwanda in Burundi★

International Socialism 2:72 Autumn 1996
Alex Callinicos: Betrayal and discontent: Labour under Blair ★ Sue Cockerill and Colin Sparks: Japan in crisis ★ Richard Levins: When science fails us ★ Ian Birchall: The Babeuf bicentenary: conspiracy or revolutionary party? ★ Brian Manning: A voice for the poor ★ Paul O'Flinn: From the kingdom of necessity to the kingdom of freedom: Morris's *News from Nowhere* ★ Clare Fermont: Bookwatch: Palestine and the Middle East 'peace process'★

International Socialism 2:71 Summer 1996
Chris Harman: The crisis of bourgeois economics ★ Hassan Mahamdallie: William Morris and revolutionary Marxism ★ Alex Callinicos: Darwin, materialism and revolution ★ Chris Nineham: Raymond Williams: revitalising the left? ★ Paul Foot: A passionate prophet of liberation ★ Gill Hubbard: Why has feminism failed women? ★ Lee Sustar: Bookwatch: fighting to unite black and white★

International Socialism 2:70 Spring 1996
Alex Callinicos: South Africa after apartheid ★ Chris Harman: France's hot December ★ Brian Richardson: The making of a revolutionary ★ Gareth Jenkins: Why Lucky Jim turned right—an obituary of Kingsley Amis ★ Mark O'Brien: The bloody birth of capitalism ★ Lee Humber: Studies in revolution ★ Adrian Budd: A new life for Lenin ★ Martin Smith: Bookwatch: the General Strike★

International Socialism 2:69 Winter 1995
Lindsey German: The Balkan war: can there be peace? ★ Duncan Blackie: The left and the Balkan war ★ Nicolai Gentchev: The myth of welfare dependency ★ Judy Cox: Wealth, poverty and class in Britain today ★ Peter Morgan: Trade unions and strikes ★ Julie Waterson: The party at its peak ★ Megan Trudell: Living to some purpose ★ Nick Howard: The rise and fall of socialism in one city ★ Andy Durgan: Bookwatch: Civil war and revolution in Spain ★

International Socialism 2:68 Autumn 1995
Ruth Brown: Racism and immigration in Britain ★ John Molyneux: Is Marxism deterministic? ★ Stuart Hood: News from nowhere? ★ Lee Sustar: Communism in the heart of the beast ★ Peter Linebaugh: To the teeth and forehead of our faults ★ George Paizis: Back to the future ★ Phil Marshall: The children of stalinism ★ Paul D'Amato: Bookwatch: 100 years of cinema ★

International Socialism 2:67 Summer 1995
Paul Foot: When will the Blair bubble burst? ★ Chris Harman: From Bernstein to Blair—100 years of revisionism ★ Chris Bambery: Was the Second World War a war for democracy? ★ Alex Callinicos: Hope against the Holocaust ★Chris Nineham: Is the media all powerful? ★ Peter Morgan: How the West was won ★ Charlie Hore: Bookwatch: China since Mao ★

International Socialism 2:66 Spring 1995
Dave Crouch: The crisis in Russia and the rise of the right ★ Phil Gasper: Cruel and unusual punishment: the politics of crime in the United States ★ Alex Callinicos: Backwards to liberalism ★

John Newsinger: Matewan: film and working class struggle ★ John Rees: The light and the dark ★ Judy Cox: How to make the Tories disappear ★ Charlie Hore: Jazz: a reply to the critics ★ Pat Riordan: Bookwatch: Ireland ★

International Socialism 2:65 Special issue
Lindsey German: Frederick Engels: life of a revolutionary ★ John Rees: Engels' Marxism ★ Chris Harman: Engels and the origins of human society ★ Paul McGarr: Engels and natural science ★

International Socialism 2:63 Summer 1994
Alex Callinicos: Crisis and class struggle in Europe today ★ Duncan Blackie: The United Nations and the politics of imperialism ★ Brian Manning: The English Revolution and the transition from feudalism to capitalism ★ Lee Sustar: The roots of multi-racial labour unity in the United States ★ Peter Linebaugh: Days of villainy: a reply to two critics ★ Dave Sherry: Trotsky's last, greatest struggle ★ Peter Morgan: Geronimo and the end of the Indian wars ★ Dave Beecham: Ignazio Silone and *Fontamara* ★ Chris Bambery: Bookwatch: understanding fascism ★

International Socialism 2:62 Spring 1994
Sharon Smith: Mistaken identity—or can identity politics liberate the oppressed? ★ Iain Ferguson: Containing the crisis—crime and the Tories ★ John Newsinger: Orwell and the Spanish Revolution ★ Chris Harman: Change at the first millenium ★ Adrian Budd: Nation and empire—Labour's foreign policy 1945-51 ★ Gareth Jenkins: Novel questions ★ Judy Cox: Blake's revolution ★ Derek Howl: Bookwatch: the Russian Revolution ★

International Socialism 2:61 Winter 1994
Lindsey German: Before the flood? ★ John Molyneux: The 'politically correct' controversy ★ David McNally: E P Thompson—class struggle and historical materialism ★ Charlie Hore: Jazz—a people's music ★ Donny Gluckstein: Revolution and the challenge of labour ★ Charlie Kimber: Bookwatch: the Labour Party in decline ★

International Socialism 2:59 Summer 1993
Ann Rogers: Back to the workhouse ★ Kevin Corr and Andy Brown: The labour aristocracy and the roots of reformism ★ Brian Manning: God, Hill and Marx ★ Henry Maitles: Cutting the wire: a criticial appraisal of Primo Levi ★ Hazel Croft: Bookwatch: women and work ★

International Socialism 2:58 Spring 1993
Chris Harman: Where is capitalism going? (part one) ★ Ruth Brown and Peter Morgan: Politics and the class struggle today: a roundtable discussion ★ Richard Greeman: The return of Comrade Tulayev: Victor Serge and the tragic vision of Stalinism ★ Norah Carlin: A new English revolution ★ John Charlton: Building a new world ★ Colin Barker: A reply to Dave McNally ★

International Socialism 2:56 Autumn 1992
Chris Harman: The Return of the National Question ★ Dave Treece: Why the Earth Summit failed ★ Mike Gonzalez: Can Castro survive? ★ Lee Humber and John Rees: The good old cause—an interview with Christopher Hill ★ Ernest Mandel: The Impasse of Schematic Dogmatism ★

International Socialism 2:55 Summer 1992
Alex Callinicos: Race and class ★ Lee Sustar: Racism and class struggle in the American Civil War era ★ Lindsey German and Peter Morgan: Prospects for socialists—an interview with Tony Cliff ★ Robert Service: Did Lenin lead to Stalin? ★ Samuel Farber: In defence of democratic revolutionary socialism ★ David Finkel: Defending 'October' or sectarian dogmatism? ★ Robin Blackburn: Reply to John Rees ★ John Rees: Dedicated followers of fashion ★ Colin Barker: In praise of custom ★ Sheila McGregor: Revolutionary witness ★

International Socialism 2:54 Spring 1992
Sharon Smith: Twilight of the American dream ★ Mike Haynes: Class and crisis—the transition in eastern Europe ★ Costas Kossis: A miracle without end? Japanese capitalism and the world economy ★ Alex Callinicos: Capitalism and the state system: A reply to Nigel Harris ★ Steven Rose: Do animals have rights? ★ John Charlton: Crime and class in the 18th century ★ John Rees: Revolution, reform and working class culture ★ Chris Harman: Blood simple ★

International Socialism 2:51 Summer 1991
Chris Harman: The state and capitalism today ★ Alex Callinicos: The end of nationalism? ★ Sharon Smith: Feminists for a strong state? ★ Colin Sparks and Sue Cockerill: Goodbye to the Swedish miracle ★ Simon Phillips: The South African Communist Party and the South African working class ★ John Brown: Class conflict and the crisis of feudalism ★

International Socialism 2:49 Winter 1990
Chris Bambery: The decline of the Western Communist Parties ★ Ernest Mandel: A theory which has not withstood the test of time ★ Chris Harman: Criticism which does not withstand the test of logic ★ Derek Howl: The law of value In the USSR ★ Terry Eagleton: Shakespeare and the class struggle ★ Lionel Sims: Rape and pre-state societies ★ Sheila McGregor: A reply to Lionel Sims ★

International Socialism 2:48 Autumn 1990
Lindsey German: The last days of Thatcher ★ John Rees: The new imperialism ★ Neil Davidson and Donny Gluckstein: Nationalism and the class struggle in Scotland ★ Paul McGarr: Order out of chaos ★

International Socialism 2:46 Winter 1989
Chris Harman: The storm breaks ★ Alex Callinicos: Can South Africa be reformed? ★ John Saville: Britain, the Marshall Plan and the Cold War ★ Sue Clegg: Against the stream ★ John Rees: The rising bourgeoisie ★

International Socialism 2:44 Autumn 1989
Charlie Hore: China: Tiananmen Square and after ★ Sue Clegg: Thatcher and the welfare state ★ John Molyneux: *Animal Farm* revisited ★ David Finkel: After Arias, is the revolution over? ★ John Rose: Jews in Poland ★

International Socialism 2:41 Winter 1988
Polish socialists speak out: Solidarity at the Crossroads ★ Mike Haynes: Nightmares of the market ★ Jack Robertson: Socialists and the unions ★ Andy Strouthous: Are the unions in decline? ★ Richard Bradbury: What is Post-Structuralism? ★ Colin Sparks: George Bernard Shaw ★

International Socialism 2:39 Summer 1988
Chris Harman and Andy Zebrowski: Glasnost, before the storm ★ Chanie Rosenberg: Labour and the fight against fascism ★ Mike Gonzalez: Central America after the Peace Plan ★ Ian Birchall: Raymond Williams ★ Alex Callinicos: Reply to John Rees ★

International Socialism 2:35 Summer 1987
Pete Green: Capitalism and the Thatcher years ★ Alex Callinicos: Imperialism, capitalism and the state today ★ Ian Birchall: Five years of *New Socialist* ★ Callinicos and Wood debate 'Looking for alternatives to reformism' ★ David Widgery replies on 'Beating Time' ★

International Socialism 2:30 Autumn 1985
Gareth Jenkins: Where is the Labour Party heading? ★ David McNally: Debt, inflation and the rate of profit ★ Ian Birchall: The terminal crisis in the British Communist Party ★ replies on Women's oppression and *Marxism Today* ★

International Socialism 2:26 Spring 1985
Pete Green: Contradictions of the American boom ★ Colin Sparks: Labour and imperialism ★ Chris Bambery: Marx and Engels and the unions ★ Sue Cockerill: The municipal road to socialism ★ Norah Carlin: Is the family part of the superstructure? ★ Kieran Allen: James Connolly and the 1916 rebellion ★

International Socialism 2:18 Winter 1983
Donny Gluckstein: Workers' councils in Western Europe ★ Jane Ure Smith: The early Communist press in Britain ★ John Newsinger: The Bolivian Revolution ★ Andy Durgan: Largo Caballero and Spanish socialism ★ M Barker and A Beezer: Scarman and the language of racism ★

International Socialism 2:14 Winter 1981
Chris Harman: The riots of 1981 ★ Dave Beecham: Class struggle under the Tories ★ Tony Cliff: Alexandra Kollontai ★ L James and A Paczuska: Socialism needs feminism ★ reply to Cliff on Zetkin ★ Feminists In the labour movement ★

DEAR GOD
the price of religion in Ireland
EAMONN McCANN

Dear God exposes the uses and abuses of religious bigotry in all its forms in Eamonn McCann's native land of Ireland. Arguments of immense seriousness are punctuated with Eamonn's tremendous wit to illuminate the absurdities of religious dogma as well as its cruelties and tragedies. This book will turn heads and aggravate bigots on both sides of the religious divide in Ireland, and everywhere religious bigotry is to be found.

'What is often overlooked about religion is something that Eamonn points his finger at immediately: it is mad. But, of course, people do still believe in it, and this book analyses this belief. The sharp mind of Eamonn McCann sorts through the mighty maze of religious beliefs, practices and paranoias for you in these pages. Hold on tight through the theological minefield. You'll be greatly entertained along the way.'

ARTHUR MATTHEWS (CO-WRITER, *FATHER TED*)

Bookmarks publication £9.99 + £1.50 p&p, available from Bookmarks, the socialist bookshop
1 Bloomsbury Street, London WC1B 3QE
Phone 020 7637 1848, fax 020 7637 3616
email bookmarks_bookshop@compuserve.com

Subscribe to

INTERNATIONAL SOCIALISM ★

Get a free copy of
'Showdown in Seattle'—the
video of the event—when
you subscribe to
International Socialism for
one year